Komm mit!

HOLT 1 GERMAN

Student Make-Up Assignments

HOLT, RINEHART AND WINSTON
A Harcourt Classroom Education Company

Austin • New York • Orlando • Atlanta • San Francisco • Boston • Dallas • Toronto • London

Contributing Writers:
Melanie Jacobs
Renate Wise

Copyright © by Holt, Rinehart and Winston

All rights reserved. No part of this publication may be reproduced or transmitted in any form or by any means, electronic or mechanical, including photocopy, recording, or any information storage and retrieval system, without permission in writing from the publisher.

Teachers using KOMM MIT! may photocopy blackline masters, in complete pages in sufficient quantities for classroom use only and not for resale.

Cover Photo/Illustration Credits:
(tl), Index Stock; (c), Network Productions/Index Stock; (br), Digital Imagery ® © 2003

KOMM MIT! is a trademark licensed to Holt, Rinehart and Winston, registered in the United States of America and/or other jurisdictions.

Printed in the United States of America

ISBN 0-03-065882-9

4 5 6 7 018 05

Table of Contents

To the Teacher v

DIAGNOSTIC INFORMATION

Kapitel 1, 2 vii
Kapitel 3, 4 viii
Kapitel 5, 6 ix
Kapitel 7, 8 x
Kapitel 9, 10 xi
Kapitel 11, 12 xii

STUDENT MAKE-UP ASSIGNMENTS CHECKLISTS

Vorschau 1
Kapitel 1 3
Kapitel 2 9
Kapitel 3 15
Kapitel 4 21
Kapitel 5 27
Kapitel 6 33
Kapitel 7 39
Kapitel 8 45
Kapitel 9 51
Kapitel 10 57
Kapitel 11 63
Kapitel 12 69

ALTERNATIVE QUIZZES

Kapitel 1
Alternative Quiz 1-1A 77
Alternative Quiz 1-2A 79
Alternative Quiz 1-3A 81

Kapitel 2
Alternative Quiz 2-1A 83
Alternative Quiz 2-2A 85
Alternative Quiz 2-3A 87

Kapitel 3
Alternative Quiz 3-1A 89
Alternative Quiz 3-2A 91
Alternative Quiz 3-3A 93

Kapitel 4
Alternative Quiz 4-1A 95
Alternative Quiz 4-2A 97
Alternative Quiz 4-3A 99

Kapitel 5
Alternative Quiz 5-1A 101
Alternative Quiz 5-2A 103
Alternative Quiz 5-3A 105

Kapitel 6
Alternative Quiz 6-1A 107
Alternative Quiz 6-2A 109
Alternative Quiz 6-3A 111

Kapitel 7

Alternative Quiz 7-1A 113
Alternative Quiz 7-2A 115
Alternative Quiz 7-3A 117

Kapitel 8

Alternative Quiz 8-1A 119
Alternative Quiz 8-2A 121
Alternative Quiz 8-3A 123

Kapitel 9

Alternative Quiz 9-1A 125
Alternative Quiz 9-2A 127
Alternative Quiz 9-3A 129

Kapitel 10

Alternative Quiz 10-1A 131
Alternative Quiz 10-2A 133
Alternative Quiz 10-3A 135

Kapitel 11

Alternative Quiz 11-1A 137
Alternative Quiz 11-2A 139
Alternative Quiz 11-3A 141

Kapitel 12

Alternative Quiz 12-1A 143
Alternative Quiz 12-2A 145
Alternative Quiz 12-3A 147

ANSWERS

Kapitel 1 151
Kapitel 2 152
Kapitel 3 153
Kapitel 4 154
Kapitel 5 155
Kapitel 6 156
Kapitel 7 157
Kapitel 8 158
Kapitel 9 159
Kapitel 10 160
Kapitel 11 161
Kapitel 12 162

To the Teacher

The blackline masters in this ancillary will help you keep track of the instructional material covered in a school year, so that you can give make-up information to students who missed class.

The first section of the book is a Diagnostic Table. In the first column of the table is a list of all the major presentations that make up the building blocks of the **Kapitel:** the functional expressions, the grammar, and the vocabulary. The activities listed in the other four columns are correlated to the **Mehr Grammatikübungen** in the *Pupil's Edition,* the **Übungsheft,** the **Grammatikheft,** and the **Interactive CD-ROM Tutor.** This table, which gives you an overview of the presentations and opportunities for practice, can also be used as a global reference for students who need extra practice in problem areas.

The second section of the book contains the Student Make-Up Assignments Checklists. These blackline masters (one for each **Stufe** of the *Pupil's Edition*) can be photocopied and given to students as make-up assignments. On the left-hand side of each blackline master is a list of the presentations in each **Stufe.** If students missed a specific presentation (or presentations), the checklist tells them what activities they can do in the **Mehr Grammatikübungen** in the *Pupil's Edition,* the **Übungsheft,** the **Grammatikheft,** or the **Interactive CD-ROM Tutor** to practice the material they missed when they were absent from class.

The third section of the book contains Alternative Quizzes that can be given to students who were absent from class when the regular Grammar and Vocabulary Quiz (Quiz A in the Testing Program) was given. The Alternative Quizzes could also be used in a different way: You can give both quizzes in the regular class, alternating rows, for example, so that students are not tempted to glance at their neighbor's paper.

The Alternative Quizzes were carefully built to reflect the same weight and level of difficulty as the regular quizzes, so that you can be assured that two students who take different versions of the quiz feel that they have been tested equally.

Diagnostic Information

The activities listed in this table are taken from the **Mehr Grammatikübungen** in the *Pupil's Edition,* the **Übungsheft,** the **Grammatikheft,** and the **CD-ROM Tutor.** They provide students with extra practice in problem areas.

Grammatik = white background; **Wortschatz** = light gray; **So sagt man das!** = dark gray

KAPITEL 1	Mehr Grammatik-übungen	Grammatikheft	Übungsheft	Interactive CD-ROM Tutor
Saying hello and goodbye		Acts. 1–2, p. 1	Acts. 2–3, p. 4	
Asking someone's name and giving yours		Acts. 3–4, p. 2		Act. 1, CD 1
Forming questions	Acts. 1–2, p. 36	Act. 5, p. 3		
Asking who someone is		Act. 6, p. 3		
The definite articles **der, die,** and **das**	Act. 3, p. 36		Acts. 4–6, p. 5	Act. 2, CD 1
Asking someone's age and giving yours		Act. 7, p. 4		
Wortschatz: The numbers 0–20		Act. 8, p. 4	Act. 7, p. 6	Act. 3, CD 1
Subject pronouns and the verb **sein**	Act. 4, p. 36	Acts. 9–10, p. 5	Acts. 8–11, pp. 6–7	Act. 4, CD 1
Talking about where people are from		Acts. 11–13, pp. 6–7	Acts. 14–15, p. 9	Act. 5, CD 1
Wortschatz: Means of transportation				Act. 6, CD 1
Talking about how someone gets to school	Acts. 6–7, p. 37	Acts. 14–16, p. 8	Acts. 12–13, p. 8	
KAPITEL 2	**Mehr Grammatik-übungen**	**Grammatikheft**	**Übungsheft**	**Interactive CD-ROM Tutor**
Wortschatz: Hobbies		Acts. 1–2, p. 10	Acts. 2–3, p. 14	Act. 1, CD 1
Subject pronoun and verb agreement	Act. 1, p. 62	Acts. 3–7, pp.10–11	Acts. 4–6, p. 15	
Subject and verb agreement	Act. 2, p. 62	Acts. 8–10, p. 12		
Wortschatz: Leisure activities and hobbies		Acts. 11–13, p.13	Acts. 9–10, p.17	Act. 2, CD 1
The present tense of verbs		Acts. 14–15, p. 14	Acts. 11–15, pp. 18–19	Act. 3, CD 1
Saying when you do various activities				Act. 4, CD 1
Wortschatz: The seasons		Act. 16, p. 15	Act. 16, p. 20	
Word order: Verb in second position	Act. 4, p. 63	Act. 17, p. 15	Acts.18–22, pp. 21–22	
Asking for an opinion and expressing yours				Act. 5, CD 1
Verbs with stems ending in **d, t,** or **n**		Acts. 18–19, p. 16		
Wortschatz: Degrees of enthusiasm		Acts. 20–22, p. 17	Act. 17, p. 20	
Agreeing and disagreeing		Acts. 23–24, p. 18		Act. 6, CD 1
Verbs that end in **-eln**	Act. 7, p. 63		Act. 25, p. 18	

German 1 Komm mit!   Student Make-Up Assignments

KAPITEL 3	Mehr Grammatik-übungen	Grammatikheft	Übungsheft	Interactive CD-ROM Tutor
Talking about where you and others live			Act. 2, p. 26	
Wortschatz: Places to live		Acts. 1–2, p. 19		
Wortschatz: Food and drink items		Act. 3, p. 20		Act. 1, CD 1
The indefinite article	Act. 2, p. 88	Acts. 6–7, p. 21		
The **möchte**-forms	Act. 1, p. 88	Act. 4, p. 20	Acts. 3–8, pp. 26–28	Act. 2, CD 1
Saying please, thank you, and you're welcome		Act. 5, p. 21		
Wortschatz: Words to describe a room		Acts. 8–10, p. 22	Act. 9, p. 29	Act. 3, CD 1
Describing a room			Acts. 10–12, pp. 29–30	
Pronouns	Act. 4, p. 89	Acts. 11–12, p. 23	Acts. 13–15, pp. 30–31	Act. 4, CD
Wortschatz: Family members		Act. 13, p. 24		
Talking about family members			Acts. 16–18, p. 32	
The possessive pronouns **mein** and **dein**	Acts. 8–9, pp. 90–91	Act. 14, p. 24		
Wortschatz: Numbers 21-100		Act. 15, p. 25		Act 5, CD 1
The possessive pronouns **sein** and **ihr**	Act. 10, p. 91	Act. 16, p. 25		
Wortschatz: Adjectives for describing people		Acts. 17–20, pp. 26–27		
Describing people			Acts. 19–23, pp. 33–34	Act. 6, CD 1
KAPITEL 4	Mehr Grammatik-übungen	Grammatikheft	Übungsheft	Interactive CD-ROM Tutor
Wortschatz: Classes at school		Acts. 1–3, p. 28	Acts. 2–3, p. 38	Act. 1, CD 1
The verb **haben**, present tense	Act. 1, p. 120	Acts. 4–6, p. 29	Acts. 4–5, p. 39	Act. 3, CD 1
Sequencing events		Acts. 7–11, p. 30	Acts. 6–8, pp. 39–40	Act. 2, CD 1
Expressing likes, dislikes, and favorites		Acts. 12–13, p. 31		
Lieblings-	Acts. 4–5, p. 121			
Responding to good news and bad news		Acts. 14–16, p. 32	Acts. 9–14, pp. 41–43	Act. 4, CD 1
Wortschatz: School supplies		Act. 17, p. 33		
Noun plurals	Acts. 6–7, p. 122	Act. 18, p. 33		Act. 5, CD 1
Talking about prices		Acts. 19–20, p. 34	Acts. 15–19, pp. 44–45	
Subject pronouns	Act. 8, pp. 122–123	Acts. 21–22, p. 35		
Pointing things out		Acts. 23–25, p. 36	Acts. 20–22, p. 46	Act. 6, CD 1

KAPITEL 5	Mehr Grammatik-übungen	Grammatikheft	Übungsheft	Interactive CD-ROM Tutor
Wortschatz: Clothes and accessories		Acts. 1–2, p. 37	Act. 2, p. 50	
Expressing wishes when shopping			Act. 3–4, pp. 50–51	
Definite and indefinite articles, accusative case	Acts. 1–2, p. 148	Acts. 3–4, p. 38	Acts. 5–7, pp. 51–52	Act. 1, CD 2
Wortschatz: Colors		Acts. 5–6, p. 39	Act. 8, p. 52	Act. 2, CD 2
Commenting on and describing clothes		Act. 7, p. 40		
Two forms of **gefallen**	Act. 4, p. 149	Act. 8, p. 40		
Wortschatz: Words to describe the fit of clothes		Act. 9, p. 41		
Giving compliments and responding to them		Act. 10, p. 41	Acts. 9–11, pp. 53–54	Act. 3, CD 2
Direct object pronouns	Act. 5, p. 149	Acts. 11–12, pp. 54–55	Acts. 12–15, pp. 42–43	Act. 4, CD 2
Talking about trying on clothes				Act. 5, CD 2
Separable-prefix verbs	Act. 8, p. 151	Acts. 13–14, p. 44	Acts. 16–19, pp. 56–57	
The stem-changing verbs **nehmen** and **aussehen**	Act. 9, p. 151	Acts. 15–16, p. 45	Acts. 20–22, pp. 57–58	Act. 6, CD 2
KAPITEL 6	Mehr Grammatik-übungen	Grammatikheft	Übungsheft	Interactive CD-ROM Tutor
Starting a conversation		Act. 1, p. 46	Act. 2, p. 62	Act. 1, CD 2
Wortschatz: Telling time		Acts. 2–5, pp. 46–47		Act. 2, CD 2
Telling time and talking about when you do things	Acts. 1–2, p. 176		Acts. 3–8, pp. 62–64	
Wortschatz: Places to go for fun		Acts. 6–8, p. 48	Acts. 9–11, p. 65	Act. 3, CD 2
The verb **wollen**	Acts. 4–6, p. 177	Acts. 9–10, p. 49	Acts. 12–14, p. 66	
Position of the conjugated verb	Act. 7, p. 178	Acts. 11–12, p. 50	Acts. 15–16, p. 67	
Wortschatz: Food and drink items at a café		Acts. 13–15, p. 51	Acts. 17–19, p. 68	Act. 4, CD 2
Stem-changing verbs	Act. 9, p. 178	Act. 16–19, pp. 52–53	Acts. 20–24, pp. 69–70	Act. 5, CD 2
Talking about how something tastes		Act. 20, p. 53		
Paying the check		Acts. 21–22, p. 54		Act. 6, CD 2

German 1 Komm mit!   Student Make-Up Assignments

KAPITEL 7	Mehr Grammatik-übungen	Grammatikheft	Übungsheft	Interactive CD-ROM Tutor
Wortschatz: Household chores		Acts. 1–2, p. 55	Acts. 2–3, p. 74	Act. 1, CD 2
The verb **müssen**	Acts. 1–2, p. 208	Acts. 3–4, p. 56	Acts. 4–8, pp. 75–76	Act. 2, CD 2
Separable prefix verbs	Act. 3, p. 208	Acts. 5–6, p. 57		
Talking about how often you have to do things			Acts. 9–10, p. 77	
Wortschatz: Time expressions		Acts. 7–8, p. 58		
Asking for and offering help, and telling someone what to do				Act. 3, CD 2
The verb **können**	Acts. 5–7, p. 209	Acts. 9–10, p. 59	Act. 11, p. 77	
The accusative pronouns	Acts. 8–9, p. 210	Acts. 11–12, p. 60	Acts. 12–14, pp. 78–79	Act. 4, CD 2
Talking about the weather		Acts. 13–14, p. 61	Acts. 15–21, pp. 80–82	Acts. 5–6, CD 2
Using present tense to express future	Act. 10, p. 211	Acts. 15–16, p. 62		
Wortschatz: Months		Acts. 17–18, p. 63		
KAPITEL 8	Mehr Grammatik-übungen	Grammatikheft	Übungsheft	Interactive CD-ROM Tutor
Wortschatz: Groceries		Acts. 1–2, p. 64	Acts. 2–4, pp. 86–87	Act. 1, CD 2
The verb **sollen**	Acts. 1–2, p. 236	Acts. 3–4, p. 65	Acts. 5–6, p. 87	
The **du**-command and the **ihr**-command	Act. 4, p. 237	Acts. 5–6, p. 66	Acts. 7–8, p. 88	Act. 2, CD 2
Wortschatz: Weights		Acts. 7–8, p. 67	Acts. 9–10, pp. 89–90	
Saying that you want something else		Acts. 9–11, p. 68	Acts. 11–14, pp. 90–91	Act. 3, CD 2
The conjunctions **denn** and **weil**	Act. 8, p. 238	Acts. 12–13, p. 69	Acts. 15–19, pp. 92–93	Act. 4, CD 2
Saying where you were and what you bought		Acts. 14–15, p. 70		Act. 6, CD 2
The past tense of **sein**	Acts. 9–10, p. 239	Acts. 16–18, pp. 71–72	Acts. 20–22, p. 94	Act. 5, CD 2

Student Make-Up Assignments

German 1 Komm mit!

Copyright © by Holt, Rinehart and Winston. All rights reserved.

KAPITEL 9	Mehr Grammatik-übungen	Grammatikheft	Übungsheft	Interactive CD-ROM Tutor
Wortschatz: Places in a city		Acts. 1–2, p. 73	Acts. 2–3, p. 98	Act. 1, CD 3
Talking about where something is located		Acts. 5–6, p. 75		
The verb **wissen**	Act. 1, p. 264	Acts. 3–4, p. 74	Acts. 4–8, pp. 99–100	Act. 2, CD 3
Wortschatz: Phrases for giving directions		Acts. 7–10, pp. 76–77		
Asking for and giving directions			Acts. 9–11, pp. 101–102	Act. 3, CD 3
Usage of **fahren** and **gehen**	Act. 4, p. 265		Acts. 12–13, p. 102	
The formal commands with **Sie**	Act. 6, p. 266	Acts. 11–12, p. 78	Acts. 14–15, p. 103	Act. 4, CD 3
Talking about what there is to eat and drink		Acts. 16–17, p. 104		
The expression **es gibt**	Act. 7, p. 266	Acts. 13–14, p. 79		
Saying you do or don't want more		Act. 15, p. 80	Act. 18, p. 105	
Accusative forms of possessives and the indefinite article	Act. 8, p. 266		Act. 19, p. 105	
Negation of indefinite articles with **kein**	Act. 9, p. 267	Acts. 16–17, p. 80	Act. 20, p. 105	Act. 5, CD 3
The conjunction **dass**	Act. 10, p. 267	Acts. 18–19, p. 81	Acts. 21–22, p. 106	Act. 6, CD 3

KAPITEL 10	Mehr Grammatik-übungen	Grammatikheft	Übungsheft	Interactive CD-ROM Tutor
Wortschatz: Film genres		Act. 1, p. 82		Act. 1, CD 3
Expressing likes and dislikes		Act. 2, p. 82	Acts. 2–4, pp. 110–111	
The verb **mögen**	Acts. 1–2, p. 296	Act. 3, p. 83	Acts. 5–8, pp. 111–112	Act. 2, CD 3
Wortschatz: Music genres		Act. 4, p. 83		
Wortschatz: Entertainers and forms of entertainment		Act. 5, p. 84		
The verb **kennen**	Act. 4, p. 297	Act. 6, p. 84		
Expressing preferences and favorites				Act. 3, CD 3
The words **lieber** and **am liebsten**	Act. 5, p. 297	Act. 7, p. 85		
The stem-changing verb **sehen**		Acts. 8–9, p. 86		
Wortschatz: Words to describe films		Acts. 10–11, p. 87	Acts. 9–15, pp. 113–115	Act. 4, CD 3
Wortschatz: Book genres		Acts. 12–14, p. 88	Acts. 16–18, pp. 116–117	Act. 5, CD 3
Stem-changing verbs	Act. 7, p. 299	Acts. 15–16, p. 89	Acts. 19–20, p. 117	Act. 6, CD 3
Talking about what you did in your free time	Act. 8, p. 299	Acts. 17–19, p. 90	Acts. 21–22, p. 118	

German 1 Komm mit! Student Make-Up Assignments

Copyright © by Holt, Rinehart and Winston. All rights reserved.

KAPITEL 11	Mehr Grammatik-übungen	Grammatikheft	Übungsheft	Interactive CD-ROM Tutor
Wortschatz: Using the telephone		Acts. 1–2, pp. 91–92		Act. 1, CD 3
Using the telephone in Germany	Act. 1, p. 324	Act. 3, p. 92	Acts. 2–7, pp. 122–124	
Inviting someone to a party and accepting or declining		Act. 4, p. 93		
Talking about birthdays and expressing good wishes	Act. 3, p. 325	Acts. 5–6, p. 94		Act. 2, CD 3
Wortschatz: Dates of the year		Acts. 7–8, p. 95		
Wortschatz: Holidays and holiday greetings			Acts. 9–15, pp. 126–127	Act. 3, CD 3
Wortschatz: Gift ideas		Act. 9, p. 96		Act. 4, CD 3
Discussing gift ideas		Act. 10, p. 96	Acts. 16–18, pp. 128–129	
Introduction to the dative case	Acts. 5–7, pp. 325–326	Acts. 11–14, pp. 97–98	Acts. 19–22, pp. 129–130	Act. 5, CD 3
Word order with dative case	Acts. 7–8, p. 326	Act. 15, p. 99		Act. 6, CD 3

KAPITEL 12	Mehr Grammatik-übungen	Grammatikheft	Übungsheft	Interactive CD-ROM Tutor
Offering help and explaining what to do			Acts. 2–7, pp. 134–136	
The preposition **für**, **du/ihr**-commands, and the verb **können**	Acts. 1–2, p. 352	Acts. 1–3, pp. 100–101		
Asking where something is located and giving directions				Act. 1, CD 3
The verb **wissen**, and the formal commands	Acts. 4–5, p. 353	Acts. 4–5, p. 102	Act. 8, p. 136	
Making plans and inviting someone to come along			Acts. 9–11, p. 137	
Wortschatz: Freetime activities		Act. 7, p. 103		Act. 2, CD 3
The verbs **wollen** and **müssen**	Act. 6, p. 353	Act. 6, p. 103	Act. 12, p. 138	Act. 3, CD 3
Talking about clothing		Acts. 8–9, p. 104		
Nominative and accusative pronouns, and definite and indefinite articles			Act. 13, p. 138	
Dative endings for **dein** and **mein**	Act. 8, p. 354	Acts. 10–11, p. 105	Acts. 14–15, p. 139	
Describing people and places		Act. 12, p. 106	Acts. 16–20, pp. 140–141	
Nominative pronouns	Act. 9, p. 354			Act. 4, CD 3
Wortschatz: Furniture and appliances		Acts. 13–15, p. 107		Act. 5, CD 3
Saying what you would like and whether you do or don't want more			Acts. 21–23, p. 142	Act. 6, CD 3
The **möchte**-forms and the use of **kein mehr**	Act. 10, p. 355	Acts. 16–17, p. 108		
Talking about what you did		Act. 18, p. 108		

Name _____ Klasse _____ Datum _____

KAPITEL V — Vorschau

■ Vorschau Student Make-Up Assignments Checklist

Pupil's Edition, pp. 1–11

The material on pp. 1–11 in the *Pupil's Edition* can best be learned and practiced in conjunction with Audio CD 1 in the Audio Program.

Study the maps of Europe, Germany, Austria, Switzerland, and Liechtenstein on pp. 1–3.	☐ Do Activity 1, p. 1 as a writing activity.
Study the map of Germany on p. 2.	☐ Do Activity 1, p. 1 in the **Übungsheft**.
Read the information on p. 5.	☐ List other native German-speakers of whom you are aware, along with some of their accomplishments.
Study **das Alphabet** on p. 6.	☐ Read the German alphabet out loud, using the rhyme presented beneath the letters to help you with correct pronunciation.
Study the conversation between the two students at the top of p. 7.	☐ After you have used context to determine what the students are saying to each other, do Activity 4c and practice introducing yourself using your new German name.
Study the picture of common classroom items on p. 8.	☐ Ask yourself, **"Was ist das?"** for each of the items shown in the picture, and answer with, **"Das ist …."** For example: **"Das ist das Fenster."** Then do Activity 2, p. 2 in the **Übungsheft**.
Study the **Ausdrücke fürs Klassenzimmer** on p. 8.	☐ Practice saying the commands and questions in German.
Study the German numbers from 0 through 20 on p. 9.	☐ Practice pronouncing the German numbers out loud, and then do Activity 3, p. 2 in the **Übungsheft**.

German 1 Komm mit!, Vorschau   Student Make-Up Assignments **1**
Copyright © by Holt, Rinehart and Winston. All rights reserved.

Name _____ Klasse _____ Datum _____

| Read the essay on p. 10. | ☐ Write down any words and phrases you can think of that the English language has borrowed from German. Do not use any of the words already listed on p. 10. |

| Read the study tips on p. 11. | ☐ List one suggestion from each box that you plan to follow during your first year of German study. |

KAPITEL 1

Name _____ Klasse _____ Datum _____

Wer bist du?

■ Erste Stufe Student Make-Up Assignments Checklist
Pupil's Edition, pp. 21–24

Study the expressions in the **So sagt man das!** box on p. 21: Saying hello and goodbye. Note that the first three greetings and the first two goodbyes are more formal than the other expressions listed.	☐ Do Activity 7, p. 22. After you have matched the exchanges with the appropriate illustrations, write whether each one is a hello or a goodbye. ☐ For additional practice, do Activities 2–3, p. 4 in the **Übungsheft** and Activities 1–2, p. 1 in the **Grammatikheft**.
Study the **So sagt man das!** box on p. 22: Asking someone's name and giving yours. You should know how to tell someone what your name is, how to ask someone their name, and how to ask about someone else's name.	☐ Do Activity 9, p. 23 as a written activity. For each illustration, fill in the part of the conversation that is not provided. ☐ For additional practice, do Activities 3–4, p. 2 in the **Grammatikheft**. ☐ For interactive practice, do Activity 1, Chapter 1, Disc 1 of the **Interactive CD-ROM Tutor**.
Study the **Grammatik** box on p. 23: Forming questions. Pay close attention to the way the verb **heißen** changes as the subject of the sentence changes.	☐ Do Activities 1–2, p. 36, **Mehr Grammatikübungen**. ☐ For additional practice, do Activity 5, p. 3 in the **Grammatikheft**.
Study the **So sagt man das!** box on p. 23: Asking who someone is. Pay attention to the question word *who?* (**wer?**) and to how the answers are phrased.	☐ Do Activity 6, p. 3 in the **Grammatikheft**.
Study the **Grammatik** box on p. 24: The definite articles **der**, **die**, and **das**. Be aware that every German noun has a gender, even words for inanimate objects.	☐ Do Activity 12, p. 24. ☐ For additional practice, do Activity 3, p. 36, **Mehr Grammatikübungen** and Activities 4–6, p. 5 in the **Übungsheft**. ☐ For interactive practice, do Activity 2, Chapter 1, Disc 1 of the **Interactive CD-ROM Tutor**.

German 1 Komm mit!, Chapter 1   Student Make-Up Assignments **3**

Name _____ Klasse _____ Datum _____

■ Erste Stufe Self-Test

Can you greet people and say goodbye?	How would you say hello and goodbye to the following people? a. a classmate b. your principal
Can you give your name and ask someone else's?	How would you introduce yourself to a new student and ask his or her name?
Can you ask and say who someone is?	How would you ask who someone is? Say who these students are. _____ Tara. _____ Jens. _____ Holger. _____ Ahmet.
Can you supply the correct definite articles (**der, die, das**) for the nouns you have learned in this chapter?	Complete Birgit's explanation to Holger about who everyone is, using the articles **der, die,** and **das**. _____ Junge da? Er heißt Helmut. Und _____ Mädchen heißt Monika. _____ Lehrer heißt Herr Becker. Und _____ Deutschlehrerin heißt Frau Hörster.

For an online self-test, go to go.hrw.com

WK3 BRANDENBURG-1

4 Student Make-Up Assignments   German 1 Komm mit!, Chapter 1

Copyright © by Holt, Rinehart and Winston. All rights reserved.

Name _____ Klasse _____ Datum _____

KAPITEL 1 — Wer bist du?

■ Zweite Stufe Student Make-Up Assignments Checklist
Pupil's Edition, pp. 25–27

Study the **So sagt man das!** box on p. 25: Asking someone's age and giving yours. Pay attention to the different verbs used in the box.	☐ Do Activity 7, p. 4 in the **Grammatikheft**.
Study the **Wortschatz** on p. 25. Read the numbers aloud and memorize them, if you have not already done so.	☐ Do Activity 16, p. 25 as a writing activity. Write both parts of the conversation between two classmates, as well as the class introduction.
	☐ For additional practice, do Activity 8, p. 4 in the **Grammatikheft** and Activity 7, p. 6 in the **Übungsheft**.
	☐ For interactive practice, do Activity 3, Chapter 1, Disc 1 of the **Interactive CD-ROM Tutor**.
Study the **Grammatik** box on p. 26: Subject pronouns and the verb **sein** *(to be)*. Learn the verb forms presented here.	☐ Do Activities 18–19, p. 26.
	☐ For additional practice, do Activity 20, p. 26, and Activity 4, p. 36, **Mehr Grammatikübungen**.
	☐ For more practice, do Activities 9–10, p. 5 in the **Grammatikheft** and Activities 8–11, pp. 6–7 in the **Übungsheft**.
	☐ For interactive practice, do Activity 4, Chapter 1, Disc 1 of the **Interactive CD-ROM Tutor**.

German 1 Komm mit!, Chapter 1   Student Make-Up Assignments **5**

Name _____ Klasse _____ Datum _____

■ Zweite Stufe Self-Test

KAPITEL 1

| Can you ask someone's age and tell yours? | How would you ask a classmate his or her age and say how old you are? |

Say how old the following students are.

Silke, 15

Dirk, 13

Marina und Susi, 14

For an online self-test, go to go.hrw.com

WK3 BRANDENBURG-1

Name _____ Klasse _____ Datum _____

KAPITEL 1

Wer bist du?

■ Dritte Stufe Student Make-Up Assignments Checklist
Pupil's Edition, pp. 28–33

Study the **So sagt man das!** box on p. 28: Talking about where people are from. You should know how to ask where others are from and to state where you (and others) come from.	☐ Do Activity 23a on p. 28 as a writing activity. Write down the name, age, and place of origin of each person pictured. ☐ For additional practice, do Activities 25 and 26c, p. 29. ☐ For more practice, do Activities 11–13, pp. 6–7 in the **Grammatikheft** and Activities 14–15, p. 9 in the **Übungsheft**. ☐ For interactive practice, do Activity 5, Chapter 1, Disc 1 of the **Interactive CD-ROM Tutor**.
Study the **Wortschatz** on p. 30. Try to derive the meanings of the sentences from context before looking up any words in the vocabulary list at the end of the chapter.	☐ Do Activity 6, Chapter 1, Disc 1 of the **Interactive CD-ROM Tutor**.
Study the **So sagt man das!** box on p. 30: Talking about how someone gets to school. You should be able to ask and answer questions relating to this subject.	☐ Do Activities 28–29, p. 32. ☐ For additional practice, do Activities 6–7, p. 37, **Mehr Grammatikübungen**. ☐ For more practice, do Activities 14–16, p. 8 in the **Grammatikheft** and Activities 12–13, p. 8 in the **Übungsheft**.

German 1 Komm mit!, Chapter 1   Student Make-Up Assignments **7**
Copyright © by Holt, Rinehart and Winston. All rights reserved.

Name _____ Klasse _____ Datum _____

■ Dritte Stufe Self-Test

KAPITEL 1

Can you ask where someone is from and tell where you are from?	How would you ask a classmate where he or she is from?
	Say where the following students are from. Make statements with both **kommen** and **sein**.
	Nicole, Brandenburg
	Britte und Andreas, Sachsen-Anhalt
	Mark, Niedersachsen
	How would you tell someone where you are from?
Can you say how someone gets to school?	How would you ask a classmate how he or she gets to school? How might he or she respond?
	Say how these people get to school:
	Steffi, bicycle
	Petra and Ali, moped
	Anna, subway

go.hrw.com For an online self-test, go to go.hrw.com

WK3 BRANDENBURG-1

8 Student Make-Up Assignments   German 1 Komm mit!, Chapter 1

Copyright © by Holt, Rinehart and Winston. All rights reserved.

Name _____ Klasse _____ Datum _____

KAPITEL 2 Spiel und Spaß

■ Erste Stufe Student Make-Up Assignments Checklist
Pupil's Edition, pp. 47–49

Study the **Wortschatz** on p. 47. Pay particular attention to word order in the various questions and statements.	☐ Do Activity 7, p. 48. ☐ For additional practice, do Activities 1–2, p. 10 in the **Grammatikheft** and Activities 2–3, p. 14 in the **Übungsheft**. ☐ For interactive practice, do Activity 1, Chapter 2, Disc 1 of the **Interactive CD-ROM Tutor**.
Study the **So sagt man das!** box on p. 48: Talking about interests. You should be able to ask what other people do in their free time, as well as describe what you and others do during free time.	☐ Do Activity 8, p. 48.
Study the **Ein wenig Grammatik** box on p. 48. Learn the verb endings corresponding to the subjects **ich, du,** and **er/sie**.	☐ Do Activity 9, p. 49. ☐ Do Activity 10, p. 49 as a writing activity. Write out a short conversation between two classmates. ☐ For additional practice, do Activity 1, p. 62, **Mehr Grammatikübungen**. ☐ For more practice, do Activities 3–7, pp. 10–11 in the **Grammatikheft** and Activities 4–6, p. 15 in the **Übungsheft**.

German 1 Komm mit!, Chapter 2   Student Make-Up Assignments

Name _____ Klasse _____ Datum _____

■ Erste Stufe Self-Test

| Can you ask about someone's interests, report them, and tell your own? | How would you ask a classmate about interests using the verbs **spielen, machen, schwimmen,** and **sammeln**? |

How would you report someone else's interests?

a. Susanne: tanzen, wandern, Gitarre spielen
b. Jörg: Golf spielen, basteln, zeichnen
c. Johannes: Schach spielen, Freunde besuchen
d. Uschi: Fernsehen schauen, Musik hören, Karten spielen

How would you tell some of the things you do?

KAPITEL 2

go.hrw.com For an online self-test, go to go.hrw.com

WK3 BRANDENBURG-2

Name _____ Klasse _____ Datum _____

KAPITEL 2 — Spiel und Spaß

■ Zweite Stufe Student Make-Up Assignments Checklist
Pupil's Edition, pp. 50–53

Study the **So sagt man das!** box on p. 50: Expressing likes and dislikes. You should be able to inquire about someone else's preferred activities and express your own.	☐ Write out a short imaginary conversation between you and a friend in which each of you asks the other what you like and don't like to do.
Study the **Ein wenig Grammatik** box on p. 50. Learn which verb endings correspond to the subjects **wir, ihr,** and **sie** (pl).	☐ Do Activity 13, p. 50. ☐ For additional practice, do Activity 2, p. 62, **Mehr Grammatikübungen**. ☐ For yet more practice, do Activities 8–10, p. 12 in the **Grammatikheft**.
Study the **Wortschatz** on p. 51. You should now know the German terms for a number of common hobbies.	☐ Do Activity 14 on p. 52. ☐ For additional practice, do Activities 11–13, p. 13 in the **Grammatikheft** and Activities 9–10, p. 17 in the **Übungsheft**. ☐ For interactive practice, do Activity 2, Chapter 2, Disc 1 of the **Interactive CD-ROM Tutor**.
Study the **Grammatik** box on p. 52: The present tense of verbs. You should now be able to adapt verbs according to this pattern.	☐ Do Activity 17, p. 53. ☐ For additional practice, do Activity 20, p. 53. ☐ For yet more practice, do Activities 14–15, p. 14 in the **Grammatikheft** and Activities 11–15, pp. 18–19 in the **Übungsheft**. ☐ For interactive practice, do Activity 3, Chapter 2, Disc 1 of the **Interactive CD-ROM Tutor**.

German 1 Komm mit!, Chapter 2

Copyright © by Holt, Rinehart and Winston. All rights reserved.

Name _____ Klasse _____ Datum _____

■ Zweite Stufe Self-Test

> Can you ask what others like to do and don't like to do, report what they say, and tell what you and your friends like and don't like to do?

How would you say what activities you like and don't like to do?

How would you ask a classmate what he or she likes to do and report that information to someone else?

How would you ask these people what they like to do and then report what they say?

Katharina und Ute: schwimmen, Schach spielen, Musik hören

How would you ask your teacher if he or she plays basketball or chess, or if he or she collects stamps?

KAPITEL 2

go.hrw.com For an online self-test, go to go.hrw.com

WK3 BRANDENBURG-2

12 Student Make-Up Assignments   German 1 Komm mit!, Chapter 2

Name _____ Klasse _____ Datum _____

KAPITEL 2 Spiel und Spaß

■ Dritte Stufe Student Make-Up Assignments Checklist
Pupil's Edition, pp. 55–59

Study the **So sagt man das!** box on p. 55: Saying when you do various activities. Jot down a list of all the time expressions used here.	☐ Do Activity 4, Chapter 2, Disc 1 of the **Interactive CD-ROM Tutor**.
Study the **Wortschatz** on p. 55, and add these terms to the list of time expressions you began above.	☐ Do Activity 23, p. 56. ☐ For additional practice, do Activities 24–25, p. 56. ☐ For more practice, do Activity 16, p. 15 in the **Grammatikheft** and Activity 16, p. 20 in the **Übungsheft**.
Study the **Grammatik** box on p. 56: Word order: Verb in second position. Compare the information in this box with what you already know about word order in questions.	☐ Do Activity 27, p. 57, as a writing activity. Write both parts of a conversation between two classmates. ☐ For additional practice, do Activity 4, p. 63, **Mehr Grammatikübungen**. ☐ For more practice, do Activity 17, p. 15 in the **Grammatikheft** and Activities 18–22, pp. 21–22 in the **Übungsheft**.
Study the **So sagt man das!** box on p. 57: Asking for an opinion and expressing yours. Notice which descriptive words are positive and which are negative.	☐ Do Activity 5, Chapter 2, Disc 1 of the **Interactive CD-ROM Tutor**.
Study the **Grammatik** box on p. 57: Verbs with stems ending in **d**, **t**, or **n**. Guess why the e is added to these verb forms.	☐ For additional practice, do Activities 18–19, p. 16 in the **Grammatikheft**.
Study the **Wortschatz** on p. 57. You should now be able to say how well you like, or how much you dislike, a certain activity.	☐ Do Activity 28, p. 57. ☐ For additional practice, do Activities 20–22, p. 17 in the **Grammatikheft** and Activity 17, p. 20 in the **Übungsheft**.

German 1 Komm mit!, Chapter 2   Student Make-Up Assignments **13**

Name _____ Klasse _____ Datum _____

Study the **So sagt man das!** box on p. 58: Agreeing and disagreeing. You should know how to quickly express agreement and disagreement in a conversation.	☐ Do Activities 23–24, p. 18 in the **Grammatikheft**. ☐ For interactive practice, do Activity 6, Chapter 2, Disc 1 of the **Interactive CD-ROM Tutor**.
Study the **Ein wenig Grammatik** box on p. 58. Notice that this rule affects only the **ich**-forms of verbs.	☐ Do Activity 31, p. 58, and Activity 33, p. 59. ☐ For additional practice, do Activity 7, p. 63, **Mehr Grammatikübungen**. ☐ For more practice, do Activity 25, p. 18 in the **Grammatikheft**.

■ Dritte Stufe Self-Test

Can you say when you do various activities?	How would you say that you a. watch TV after school b. play soccer in the afternoon c. go hiking in the spring d. swim in the summer
Can you ask for an opinion, agree, disagree, and express your own opinion?	How would you ask a classmate what he or she thinks of a. tennis c. drawing b. music d. hiking Agree or disagree with the following statements. If you disagree, express your opinion. a. Schach ist langweilig. b. Basteln macht Spaß. c. Briefmarkensammeln ist interessant. d. Tennis ist super! How would you express your opinion of the following activities: a. Fußball spielen c. wandern b. Briefmarken sammeln d. schwimmen

go.hrw.com For an online self-test, go to go.hrw.com

WK3 BRANDENBURG-2

KAPITEL 3 — Komm mit nach Hause!

Name _____ Klasse _____ Datum _____

■ Erste Stufe   Student Make-Up Assignments Checklist
Pupil's Edition, pp. 73–76

Study the **So sagt man das!** box on p. 73: Talking about where you and others live. You should be able to ask and tell where people live.	☐ Do Activity 2, p. 26 in the **Übungsheft**.
Study the **Wortschatz** on p. 73. Read each statement aloud and make sure you understand what it means.	☐ Do Activity 7, p. 74. ☐ For additional practice, do Activity 8, p. 74 as a writing activity. Write both parts of an imaginary conversation between you and a classmate. ☐ For more practice, do Activities 1–2, p. 19 in the **Grammatikheft**.
Study the **So sagt man das!** box on p. 74: Offering something to eat and drink and responding to an offer. Practice reading the questions and answers aloud.	☐ Write out all the unfamiliar German vocabulary in the box and guess what each word means using context clues. After you have done this, look up each word in the **Wortschatz** on p. 95 and check your guesses.
Study the **Wortschatz** on p. 75. Notice how many of the German words are similar to their English equivalents.	☐ Do Activity 9, p. 75 as a writing activity. ☐ For additional practice, do Activity 3, p. 20 in the **Grammatikheft**. ☐ For interactive practice, do Activity 1, Chapter 3, Disc 1 of the **Interactive CD-ROM Tutor**.
Study the **Ein wenig Grammatik** box on p. 75. How do these indefinite articles correspond to the definite articles you learned earlier (**der, die, das**)?	☐ Do Activity 10, p. 75 as a writing activity. Do part a. as a written activity. ☐ For additional practice, do Activity 2, p. 88, **Mehr Grammatikübungen**. ☐ For more practice, do Activities 6–7, p. 21 in the **Grammatikheft**.
Study the **Grammatik** box on p. 76: The **möchte**-forms. It is very important that you learn these forms.	☐ Do Activity 11, p. 76. ☐ For additional practice, do Activity 1, p. 88, **Mehr Grammatikübungen**. ☐ For more practice, do Activity 4, p. 20 in the **Grammatikheft** and Activities 3–8, pp. 26–28 in the **Übungsheft**. ☐ For interactive practice, do Activity 2, Chapter 3, Disc 1 of the **Interactive CD-ROM Tutor**.

German 1 Komm mit!, Chapter 3   Student Make-Up Assignments

Name _____ Klasse _____ Datum _____

| Study the **So sagt man das!** box on p. 76: Saying please, thank you, and you're welcome. Practice saying the words in a conversational tone. | ☐ Do Activity 5, p. 21 in the **Grammatikheft**. |

■ Erste Stufe Self-Test

Can you talk about where people live?	How would you ask a classmate where he or she lives and tell him or her where you live? Say where the following people live:
	a. Thomas (Land)
	b. Britte (Hegelstraße)
	c. Marian und Karl (Brauhausberg, Vorort von Potsdam)
	d. Renate (Köln)
	e. Sabine und Rolf (Stadt: Bismarckstr.)
Can you offer something to eat and drink (using **möchte**) and respond to an offer?	How would you ask a classmate what he or she would like to eat and drink? How would you ask more than one classmate? How would you tell a classmate that you would like a lemon-flavored soda?
	If you and some of your classmates were at a friend's house, how would you help your friend by telling her or him what everyone was having for a snack?
	a. Anna, eine Cola
	b. Martin und Klaus, ein Stück Kuchen
	c. Nicole und Jörg, ein paar Kekse
	d. Ayla, Obst
Can you say please, thank you, and you're welcome?	How would you ask your friend politely for a few cookies? How would you thank him or her? How would he or she respond?

go.hrw.com For an online self-test, go to **go.hrw.com**

WK3 BRANDENBURG-3

KAPITEL 3

Name _____ Klasse _____ Datum _____

Komm mit nach Hause!

■ Zweite Stufe Student Make-Up Assignments Checklist
Pupil's Edition, pp. 78–80

Study the **Wortschatz** on p. 78. Try to guess what the German words in the oval at the bottom of the box mean. (the word pairs are opposite)	☐ Do Activities 8–10, p. 22 in the **Grammatikheft**. ☐ For additional practice, do Activity 9, p. 29 in the **Übungsheft**. ☐ For interactive practice, do Activity 3, Chapter 3, Disc 1 of the **Interactive CD-ROM Tutor**.
Study the **So sagt man das!** box on p. 79: Describing a room. You should know how to describe basic furniture items in terms of their comfort and appearance.	☐ Do Activity 14, p. 79. ☐ For additional practice, do Activities 10–12, pp. 29–30 in the **Übungsheft**.
Study the **Grammatik** box on p. 79: Pronouns. Practice saying the alternate forms of the sentences out loud.	☐ Do Activities 16–17, p. 80. For Activity 17, write out both parts of an imaginary conversation between you and a classmate. ☐ For additional practice, do Activity 4, p. 89, **Mehr Grammatikübungen**. ☐ For more practice, do Activities 11–12, p. 23 in the **Grammatikheft** and Activities 13–15, pp. 30–31 in the **Übungsheft**. ☐ For interactive practice, do Activity 4, Chapter 3, Disc 1 of the **Interactive CD-ROM Tutor**.

German 1 Komm mit!, Chapter 3   Student Make-Up Assignments

Name _____ Klasse _____ Datum _____

■ Zweite Stufe Self-Test

| Can you describe a room? | How would you describe these pieces of furniture? Make two sentences about each one using the correct pronoun **er, sie, es,** or **sie** (pl) in the second sentence.
a. der Schrank *(old, ugly, large)*
b. das Bett *(small, comfortable, new)*
c. die Möbel *(beautiful, new, large)*
d. die Couch *(old, ugly, broken)* |

For an online self-test, go to **go.hrw.com**

WK3 BRANDENBURG-3

KAPITEL 3

Name _____ Klasse _____ Datum _____

Komm mit nach Hause!

■ Dritte Stufe Student Make-Up Assignments Checklist
Pupil's Edition, pp. 81–85

Study the **Wortschatz** on p. 81. Try mentally filling in your own family members' names as you go through the family tree.	☐ Do Activity 19, p. 81. ☐ For additional practice, do Activity 13, p. 24 in the **Grammatikheft**.
Study the **So sagt man das!** box on p. 82: Talking about family members. You should be able to talk about the names, ages, and residences of your family members.	☐ Do Activities 16–18, p. 32 in the **Übungsheft**.
Study the **Ein wenig Grammatik** box on p. 82. Learn these two possessives.	☐ Do Activity 21, p. 82. ☐ For additional practice, do Activities 8–9, pp. 90–91, **Mehr Grammatikübungen**. ☐ For more practice, do Activity 14, p. 24 in the **Grammatikheft**.
Study the **Wortschatz** on p. 83. You should now be able to count from 0 to 100.	☐ Do Activity 15, p. 25 in the **Grammatikheft**. ☐ For interactive practice, do Activity 5, Chapter 3, Disc 1 of the **Interactive CD-ROM Tutor**.
Study the **Ein wenig Grammatik** box on p. 83. Commit these two possessives to memory.	☐ Do Activity 23, p. 83 as a writing activity. Write a short, imaginary conversation between you and a classmate. ☐ For additional practice, do Activity 10, p. 91, **Mehr Grammatikübungen**. ☐ For more practice, do Activity 16, p. 25 in the **Grammatikheft**.
Study the **Wortschatz** on p. 84. Read the descriptions aloud, figuring out as much vocabulary as you can from context.	☐ Do Activity 25, p. 84. ☐ For additional practice, do Activities 17–20, pp. 26–27 in the **Grammatikheft**.
Study the **So sagt man das!** box on p. 84: Describing people. You should be able to ask and answer questions about people's appearance.	☐ Do Activity 26, p. 85. ☐ For additional practice, do Activities 19–23, pp. 33–34 in the **Übungsheft**. ☐ For interactive practice, do Activity 6, Chapter 3, Disc 1 of the **Interactive CD-ROM Tutor**.

German 1 Komm mit!, Chapter 3

Name _____ Klasse _____ Datum _____

■ Dritte Stufe Self-Test

Can you talk about family members?	How would you tell a classmate about five of your family members, giving their relationship to you, their names, and their ages?
Can you describe people?	How would you describe these people? a. an older white woman with short white hair and blue eyes b. an older dark-skinned man, bald, wears glasses and has brown eyes c. a young man with short black hair and brown eyes d. a young woman with short red hair and green eyes How would you ask a classmate what his or her brother, sister, grandfather, parents, and cousins (male and female) look like?

For an online self-test, go to go.hrw.com

WK3 BRANDENBURG-3

KAPITEL 3

20 Student Make-Up Assignments

German 1 Komm mit!, Chapter 3

Copyright © by Holt, Rinehart and Winston. All rights reserved.

KAPITEL 4

Name _____ Klasse _____ Datum _____

Alles für die Schule!

■ Erste Stufe Student Make-Up Assignments Checklist
Pupil's Edition, pp. 105–109

Study the **Wortschatz** on p. 105. As you read through the schedule, try to guess what the unfamiliar words mean.	☐ Do Activity 6, p. 105. ☐ For additional practice, do Activity 7, p. 106. ☐ For more practice, do Activities 1–3, p. 28 in the **Grammatikheft** and Activities 2–3, p. 38 in the **Übungsheft**. ☐ For interactive practice, do Activity 1, Chapter 4, Disc 1 of the **Interactive CD-ROM Tutor**.
Study the **So sagt man das!** box on p. 106: Talking about class schedules. You should be able to ask about the classes being taken by others, and to tell about your own and other people's classes.	☐ Do Activity 8, p. 106 as a writing activity. Write a short paragraph in German that describes your class schedule. Use complete sentences.
Study the **So sagt man das!** box on p. 107: Using a schedule to talk about time. You should be able to ask and talk about when something happens.	☐ Do Activity 11, p. 108 as a writing activity. Write out an imaginary conversation between two classmates.
Study the **Grammatik** box on p. 108: The verb **haben**, present tense. You must memorize these verb forms.	☐ Do Activity 12, p. 108. ☐ For additional practice, do Activity 1, p. 120, **Mehr Grammatikübungen**. ☐ For more practice, do Activities 4–6, p. 29 in the **Grammatikheft** and Activities 4–5, p. 39 in the **Übungsheft**. ☐ For interactive practice, do Activity 3, Chapter 4, Disc 1 of the **Interactive CD-ROM Tutor**.
Study the **So sagt man das!** box on p. 109: Sequencing events. You should know how to list events chronologically.	☐ Do Activity 14, p. 109 as a writing activity. ☐ For additional practice, do Activity 15, p. 109 as a writing activity, and Activity 16, p. 109. ☐ For more practice, do Activities 7–11, p. 30 in the **Grammatikheft** and Activities 6–8, pp. 39–40 in the **Übungsheft**. ☐ For interactive practice, do Activity 2, Chapter 4, Disc 1 of the **Interactive CD-ROM Tutor**.

German 1 Komm mit!, Chapter 4   Student Make-Up Assignments
Copyright © by Holt, Rinehart and Winston. All rights reserved.

Name _____ Klasse _____ Datum _____

Erste Stufe Self-Test

KAPITEL 4

Can you talk about schedules using **haben**?	How would you say the following in German:
	a. Ulrike has German on Wednesday and Friday.
	b. Monika and Klaus have history on Tuesday and Thursday.
	c. Richard has no classes on Saturday.
	How would you ask a friend what classes he or she has on Monday? How might he or she respond? How would you ask two friends? How might they respond if they both have the same schedule?
Can you use a schedule to talk about time?	Say when these people have these classes.
	a. Martin, 8.30 Mathe
	b. Claudia und Ingrid, 9.45 Latein
	c. Heiko, 10.20 Musik
	d. Michaela und Manfred, 3.00 Kunst
	How would you tell someone what time you have your German class, using the expression **von ... bis ...**?
Can you sequence events using **zuerst, dann, danach,** and **zuletzt**?	How would you tell a classmate the sequence of your classes on Thursday?

For an online self-test, go to go.hrw.com

WK3 SCHLESWIG-HOLSTEIN-4

Name _____ Klasse _____ Datum _____

KAPITEL 4 — Alles für die Schule!

■ Zweite Stufe Student Make-Up Assignments Checklist
Pupil's Edition, pp. 110–112

Study the **So sagt man das!** box on p. 110: Expressing likes, dislikes, and favorites. Read through the questions and responses aloud.	☐ Do Activities 12–13, p. 31 in the **Grammatikheft**.
Study the **Ein wenig Grammatik** box on p. 110. Can you create any additional compound words using **Lieblings-** and vocabulary you have already learned?	☐ Do Activity 18, p. 110 as a writing activity. Fill out the chart and write a report discussing the likes and dislikes of an imaginary classmate. ☐ For additional practice, do Activities 4–5, p. 121, **Mehr Grammatikübungen**.
Study the **So sagt man das!** box on p. 112: Responding to good news and bad news. Read the questions and answers aloud as though you were taking part in a conversation.	☐ Do Activity 21, p. 112. ☐ For additional practice, do Activity 23, p. 112. ☐ For more practice, do Activities 14–16, p. 32 in the **Grammatikheft** and Activities 9–14, pp. 41–43 in the **Übungsheft**. ☐ For interactive practice, do Activity 4, Chapter 4, Disc 1 of the **Interactive CD-ROM Tutor**.

German 1 Komm mit!, Chapter 4 — Student Make-Up Assignments **23**

Copyright © by Holt, Rinehart and Winston. All rights reserved.

Name _____ Klasse _____ Datum _____

■ Zweite Stufe Self-Test

KAPITEL 4

Can you express likes, dislikes, and favorites?	How would you say which subjects you like, dislike, and which is your favorite? How would you ask your friend for the same information?
Can you respond to good news and bad news?	How would you respond if Ahmet, an exchange student at your school, told you: a. Ich habe eine Eins in Bio. b. Ich habe eine Vier in Latein. c. Ich habe eine Zwei in Englisch.

go.hrw.com For an online self-test, go to go.hrw.com

WK3 SCHLESWIG-HOLSTEIN-4

Name _____ Klasse _____ Datum _____

KAPITEL 4

Alles für die Schule!

■ Dritte Stufe Student Make-Up Assignments Checklist
Pupil's Edition, pp. 114–117

Study the **Wortschatz** on p. 114. Try to guess what the new vocabulary means before looking up the words.	☐ Do Activity 24, p. 114 as a writing activity. Skip the step in which you compare your list with a classmate's. ☐ For additional practice, do Activity 17, p. 33 in the **Grammatikheft**.
Study the **Grammatik** box on p. 114: Noun plurals. Write the sentences suggested at the end of the box.	☐ Do Activities 6–7, p. 122, **Mehr Grammatikübungen**. ☐ For additional practice, do Activity 18, p. 33 in the **Grammatikheft**. ☐ For interactive practice, do Activity 5, Chapter 4, Disc 1 of the **Interactive CD-ROM Tutor**.
Study the **So sagt man das!** box on p. 115: Talking about prices. You should know how to ask about prices, give prices, and comment on prices.	☐ Do Activities 19–20, p. 34 in the **Grammatikheft**. ☐ For additional practice, do Activities 15–19, pp. 44–45 in the **Übungsheft**.
Look at the **Ein wenig Grammatik (Schon bekannt)** box on p. 115. This box reviews material you learned in Chapter 3.	☐ If any of the information presented here looks unfamiliar to you, review the **Grammatik** box on p. 79. ☐ Do Activity 8, pp. 122–123, **Mehr Grammatikübungen**. ☐ For additional practice, do Activities 21–22, p. 35 in the **Grammatikheft**. ☐ For more practice, do Activity 26, p. 116 as a writing activity.
Study the **So sagt man das!** box on p. 116: Pointing things out. You should know how to indicate where things are located in a store.	☐ Do Activity 27, p. 116. ☐ For additional practice, do Activities 23–25, p. 36 in the **Grammatikheft** and Activities 20–22, p. 46 in the **Übungsheft**. ☐ For interactive practice, do Activity 6, Chapter 4, Disc 1 of the **Interactive CD-ROM Tutor**.

German 1 Komm mit!, Chapter 4   Student Make-Up Assignments

Name _____ Klasse _____ Datum _____

Dritte Stufe Self-Test

Can you talk about prices?	How would you ask a salesperson how much these items cost: calculators, notebooks, erasers, pencils, pens, school bags, dictionaries, and cassettes?
	How would you tell your friend what each of the following items costs? How might he or she comment on the prices? a. Wörterbuch: Euro 18,00 b. Kuli: Euro 3,20 c. Schultasche: Euro 24,00
Can you point things out?	Write a conversation in which your friend asks you where several things are located in a store. You point them out and give a general location. Then tell him or her how much they cost.

For an online self-test, go to go.hrw.com

WK3 SCHLESWIG-HOLSTEIN-4

Name _____ Klasse _____ Datum _____

KAPITEL 5 Klamotten kaufen

■ Erste Stufe Student Make-Up Assignments Checklist
Pupil's Edition, pp. 133–136

Study the **Wortschatz** on p. 133. Read each word aloud and make sure you understand what it means.	☐ Do Activity 7, p. 134 as a writing activity. Create a price list and then write a short, imaginary conversation between two classmates.
	☐ For additional practice, do Activity 8, p. 134.
	☐ For more practice, do Activities 1–2, p. 37 in the **Grammatikheft** and Activity 2, p. 50 in the **Übungsheft**.
Study the **So sagt man das!** box on p. 134: Expressing wishes when shopping. You should be able to ask what type of clothing item someone wants and tell what type of clothing item you would like.	☐ Do Activities 3–4, pp. 50–51 in the **Übungsheft**.
Study the **Grammatik** box on p. 135: Definite and indefinite articles, accusative case. You must understand what subjects and direct objects are and how to form them in German.	☐ Do Activity 10, p. 135, and Activity 11, p. 135 as a writing activity.
	☐ For additional practice, do Activities 1–2, p. 148, **Mehr Grammatikübungen**.
	☐ For more practice, do Activities 3–4, p. 38 in the **Grammatikheft** and Activities 5–7, pp. 51–52 in the **Übungsheft**.
	☐ For interactive practice, do Activity 1, Chapter 5, Disc 2 of the **Interactive CD-ROM Tutor**.
Study the **Wortschatz** on p. 136. Read the names of the colors aloud until you can pronounce them fluently.	☐ Do Activity 13, p. 136 as a writing activity. Write out a conversation between yourself and a salesperson.
	☐ For additional practice, do Activities 5–6, p. 39 in the **Grammatikheft**, and Activity 8, p. 52 in the **Übungsheft**.
	☐ For interactive practice, do Activity 2, Chapter 5, Disc 2 of the **Interactive CD-ROM Tutor**.

German 1 Komm mit!, Chapter 5   Student Make-Up Assignments

Name _____ Klasse _____ Datum _____

■ Erste Stufe Self-Test

| Can you express wishes when shopping? | How would a salesperson in a clothing store ask what you would like? |

How would you answer, saying that you were looking for the following? (Be sure to practice using the articles correctly, and watch out for direct objects.)

a. a sweater
b. boots in black
c. pants in red
d. a shirt in brown
e. a jacket in light gray
f. a dress in blue

KAPITEL 6

For an online self-test, go to go.hrw.com

WK3 SCHLESWIG-HOLSTEIN-5

28 Student Make-Up Assignments   German 1 Komm mit!, Chapter 5

Name _____ Klasse _____ Datum _____

KAPITEL 5 — Klamotten kaufen

■ Zweite Stufe Student Make-Up Assignments Checklist
Pupil's Edition, pp. 137–141

Study the **So sagt man das!** box on p. 137: Commenting on and describing clothes. You should be able to ask someone's opinion of clothes, and to make positive, negative, and uncertain comments about clothes.	☐ Do Activity 7, p. 40 in the **Grammatikheft**.
Study the **Ein wenig Grammatik** box on p. 137. Learn these two forms of **gefallen**, as well as how to use them in sentences.	☐ Do Activity 16, p. 138 as a writing activity. Write a conversation between two classmates. ☐ For additional practice, do Activity 4, p. 149, **Mehr Grammatikübungen**. ☐ For more practice, do Activity 8, p. 40 in the **Grammatikheft**.
Study the **Wortschatz** on p. 138. Read the sentences out loud and make sure you understand what they mean.	☐ Do Activity 17, p. 139 as a writing activity. ☐ For additional practice, do Activity 9, p. 41 in the **Grammatikheft**.
Study the **So sagt man das!** box on p. 139: Giving compliments and responding to them. You should know how to make favorable comments about clothes and how to respond to such comments.	☐ Do Activity 18a, p. 139. ☐ For additional practice, do Activity 10, p. 41 in the **Grammatikheft** and Activities 9–11, pp. 53–54 in the **Übungsheft**. ☐ For interactive practice, do Activity 3, Chapter 5, Disc 2 of the **Interactive CD-ROM Tutor**.
Study the **Grammatik** box on p. 140: Direct object pronouns. Create your own chart, matching these pronouns to their subject (nominative) forms.	☐ Do Activities 20–21, p. 141 as writing activities. ☐ For additional practice, do Activity 5, p. 149, **Mehr Grammatikübungen**. ☐ For more practice, do Activities 11–12, pp. 42–43 in the **Grammatikheft** and Activities 12–15, pp. 54–55 in the **Übungsheft**. ☐ For interactive practice, do Activity 4, Chapter 5, Disc 2 of the **Interactive CD-ROM Tutor**.

German 1 Komm mit!, Chapter 5   Student Make-Up Assignments **29**

Name _____ Klasse _____ Datum _____

■ Zweite Stufe Self-Test

Can you comment on and describe clothing?	How would you ask a friend what he or she thinks of these clothes:

a. a jacket
b. a pair of shoes
c. a jogging suit
d. a shirt

How might your friend respond positively? Negatively? With uncertainty?

How would you disagree with the following statements by saying the opposite? Use the correct pronoun.

a. The jacket is too short.
b. The shoes are too tight.
c. The jogging suit is too small.
d. The shirt fits just right.
e. I think the belt is terrible.
f. I like the tennis shoes.
g. I think the dress is too long.
h. The skirt looks stylish.

Can you compliment someone's clothing and respond to compliments?	How would you compliment Katja, using the cues below?

a. blouse   c. T-shirt
b. sweater   d. skirt

How might Katja respond to your compliments? What would you say next?

go.hrw.com For an online self-test, go to go.hrw.com

WK3 SCHLESWIG-HOLSTEIN-5

30 Student Make-Up Assignments   German 1 Komm mit!, Chapter 5

Copyright © by Holt, Rinehart and Winston. All rights reserved.

Name _____ Klasse _____ Datum _____

KAPITEL 5

Klamotten kaufen

■ Dritte Stufe Student Make-Up Assignments Checklist
Pupil's Edition, pp. 143–145

Study the **So sagt man das!** box on p. 143: Talking about trying on clothes. Know how to say that you are trying on a clothing item and whether or not you intend to buy it.	☐ Do Activity 5, Chapter 5, Disc 2 of the **Interactive CD-ROM Tutor**.
Study the **Grammatik** box on p. 143: Separable-prefix verbs. Practice using the verbs in different sentences.	☐ Do Activity 24, p. 144. ☐ For additional practice, do Activity 8, p. 151, **Mehr Grammatikübungen**. ☐ For more practice, do Activities 13–14, p. 44 in the **Grammatikheft** and Activities 16–19, pp. 56–57 in the **Übungsheft**.
Study the **Ein wenig Grammatik** box on p. 144. Memorize the verb forms shown in the box.	☐ Do Activities 25–26, p. 144 as writing activities. ☐ For additional practice, do Activity 9, p. 151, **Mehr Grammatikübungen**. ☐ For more practice, do Activities 15–16, p. 45 in the **Grammatikheft** and Activities 20–22, pp. 57–58 in the **Übungsheft**. ☐ For interactive practice, do Activity 6, Chapter 5, Disc 2 of the **Interactive CD-ROM Tutor**.

KAPITEL 5

German 1 Komm mit!, Chapter 5   Student Make-Up Assignments **31**
Copyright © by Holt, Rinehart and Winston. All rights reserved.

Name _____ Klasse _____ Datum _____

■ Dritte Stufe Self-Test

Can you talk about trying on clothes?

How would you tell a friend what the following people are wearing to Sonja's party? (Remember to use **anziehen!**)

a. Julia

b. Katja

c. Heiko

How would you tell the salesperson that you would like to try on a shirt in red, pants in white, a sweater in yellow, and a jacket in brown?

How would you tell your friend that you will get the shirt, the sweater, and the jacket? (Use **nehmen** or **kaufen**.)

KAPITEL 5

For an online self-test, go to go.hrw.com

WK3 SCHLESWIG-HOLSTEIN-5

Name _____ Klasse _____ Datum _____

KAPITEL 6 Pläne machen

■ Erste Stufe Student Make-Up Assignments Checklist
Pupil's Edition, pp. 161–164

Study the **So sagt man das!** box on p. 161: Starting a conversation. You should know how to begin an informal conversation with someone.	☐ Do Activity 8, p. 161 as a writing activity. Write a conversation between two classmates, integrating the times shown on the watch faces.
	☐ For additional practice, do Activity 1, p. 46 in the **Grammatikheft** and Activity 2, p. 62 in the **Übungsheft**.
	☐ For interactive practice, do Activity 1, Chapter 6, Disc 2 of the **Interactive CD-ROM Tutor**.
Study the **Wortschatz** on p. 162. Practice reading the times aloud.	☐ Do Activity 10, p. 162 and then do Activity 11, p. 163 as a writing activity. Instead of writing a conversation for Activity 11, write out both the formal and informal ways of stating the times shown on the clock faces.
	☐ For additional practice, do Activities 2–5, pp. 46–47 in the **Grammatikheft**.
	☐ For interactive practice, do Activity 2, Chapter 6, Disc 2 of the **Interactive CD-ROM Tutor**.
Study the **So sagt man das!** box on p. 162: Telling time and talking about when you do things. You should now be able to integrate times into your conversations.	☐ Do Activity 12, p. 163 as a writing activity, and then do Activity 14, p. 164.
	☐ For additional practice, do Activities 1–2, p. 176, **Mehr Grammatikübungen**.
	☐ For more practice, do Activities 3–8, pp. 62–64 in the **Übungsheft**.

German 1 Komm mit!, Chapter 6

Name _____ Klasse _____ Datum _____

■ Erste Stufe Self-Test

Can you start a conversation?	How would you greet a friend and ask how he or she is doing? If someone asks how you are doing, what could you say?
Can you tell time?	How would you ask what time it is? Say the times shown below, using expressions you learned in this chapter. a. 1.00 b. 11.30 c. 9.50 d. 2.15 e. 7.55
Can you talk about when you do things?	Using the time expressions above, say when you and your friends intend to a. go to the movies b. go to a café c. go to the swimming pool How would you ask a friend when he intends to do the activities above?

For an online self-test, go to go.hrw.com

WK3 SCHLESWIG-HOLSTEIN-6

KAPITEL 6

Name _____ Klasse _____ Datum _____

Pläne machen

■ Zweite Stufe Student Make-Up Assignments Checklist
Pupil's Edition, pp. 165–168

Study the **Wortschatz** on p. 165. Read the sentences aloud until you can say each one fluently. Try to guess from context the meanings of any unfamiliar words.	☐ Do Activities 17–18, p. 165. ☐ For additional practice, do Activities 6–8, p. 48 in the **Grammatikheft** and Activities 9–11, p. 65 in the **Übungsheft**. ☐ For interactive practice, do Activity 3, Chapter 6, Disc 2 of the **Interactive CD-ROM Tutor**.
Study the **So sagt man das!** box on p. 166: Making plans. If necesssary, review the **möchte**-forms.	☐ Do Activity 23, p. 168. As you read the letter, see how many different forms of the verb **wollen** you can spot. Match the forms with their subjects, and then go on with the activity. ☐ For additional practice, do Activity 24, p. 168.
Study the **Grammatik** box on p. 166: The verb **wollen**. Learn these verb forms.	☐ Do Activity 19, p. 166, and Activity 20, p. 167. ☐ For additional practice, do Activities 4–6, p. 177, **Mehr Grammatikübungen**. ☐ For more practice, do Activities 9–10, p. 49 in the **Grammatikheft** and Activities 12–14, p. 66 in the **Übungsheft**.
Look at the **Ein wenig Grammatik (Schon bekannt)** box on p. 167. This box reviews material you learned in Chapter 2.	☐ If any of the information presented here looks unfamiliar to you, review the **Grammatik** box on p. 56. ☐ Do Activity 7, p. 178, **Mehr Grammatikübungen**. ☐ For additional practice, do Activities 11–12, p. 50 in the **Grammatikheft** and Activities 15–16, p. 67 in the **Übungsheft**.

German 1 Komm mit!, Chapter 6   Student Make-Up Assignments **35**

Name _____ Klasse _____ Datum _____

■ Zweite Stufe Self-Test

Can you make plans using wollen?

Say you intend to go to the following places and tell what you plan to do there. Establish a sequence: *first..., then....*

a. café
b. swimming pool
c. movies
d. department store
e. disco

How would you say that the following people want to go to a concert?

a. Michael
b. Silke
c. ihr
d. wir
e. Peter und Monika

For an online self-test, go to go.hrw.com

WK3 SCHLESWIG-HOLSTEIN-6

KAPITEL 6 Pläne machen

Name _____ Klasse _____ Datum _____

■ Dritte Stufe Student Make-Up Assignments Checklist
Pupil's Edition, pp. 170–173

Study the **So sagt man das!** box on p. 170: Ordering food and beverages. You should now know several different verbs to use when ordering food.	☐ Do Activity 26, p. 170 as a writing activity. Use complete sentences to write down what you would like to eat and drink, and then add up your total bill.
Study the **Wortschatz** on p. 171. Read the new vocabulary words aloud.	☐ Do Activity 28, p. 171 as a writing activity. Write an imaginary conversation between yourself and a waiter.
	☐ For additional practice, do Activities 13–15, p. 51 in the **Grammatikheft** and Activities 17–19, p. 68 in the **Übungsheft**.
	☐ For interactive practice, do Activity 4, Chapter 6, Disc 2 of the **Interactive CD-ROM Tutor**.
Study the **Grammatik** box on p. 171: Stem-changing verbs. Learn the forms of **essen**.	☐ Do Activity 29, p. 171 as a writing activity. Write out in complete sentences what you and a friend would like to eat.
	☐ For additional practice, do Activity 9, p. 178, **Mehr Grammatikübungen**.
	☐ For more practice, do Activities 16–19, pp. 52–53 in the **Grammatikheft**, and Activities 20–24, pp. 69–70 in the **Übungsheft**.
	☐ For interactive practice, do Activity 5, Chapter 6, Disc 2 of the **Interactive CD-ROM Tutor**.

German 1 Komm mit!, Chapter 6   Student Make-Up Assignments

Name _____ Klasse _____ Datum _____

Study the **So sagt man das!** box on p. 172: Talking about how something tastes. You should be able to ask and tell someone how something tastes.	☐ Do Activity 30, part 1, p. 172 as a writing activity. ☐ For additional practice, do Activity 20, p. 53 in the **Grammatikheft**.
Study the **So sagt man das!** box on p. 172: Paying the check. You should know how to get the waiter's attention, pay the check, and leave the waiter a tip.	☐ Do Activity 32, p. 172 as a writing activity. Choose one of the orders listed and write out your conversation with the waiter. ☐ For additional practice, do Activities 21–22, p. 54 in the **Grammatikheft**. ☐ For interactive practice, do Activity 6, Chapter 6, Disc 2 of the **Interactive CD-ROM Tutor**.

■ Dritte Stufe Self-Test

Can you order food and beverages?	You are with some friends in a café. Order the following things for yourself. a. (noodle) soup b. a glass of tea with lemon c. a cheese sandwich Say that these people are going to eat the foods listed. Then say what you are going to eat (using **ich**). How would you ask your best friend what he or she is going to eat (using **du**)? a. Michael: Käsekuchen b. Holger und Julia: Apfelkuchen c. Monika: Käsebrot d. Ahmet und ich: Wiener mit Senf e. Ich … f. Und du? Was …?
Can you talk about how something tastes?	How would you ask a friend if his or her food tastes good? How might he or she respond?
Can you pay the check?	Ask the waiter for the check, and then tell him to keep the change.

For an online self-test, go to go.hrw.com

WK3 SCHLESWIG-HOLSTEIN-6

KAPITEL 7 Zu Hause helfen

Name _____ Klasse _____ Datum _____

■ Erste Stufe Student Make-Up Assignments Checklist
Pupil's Edition, pp. 193–196

Study the **Wortschatz** on p. 193. Read the new vocabulary out loud and use the pictures to figure out what unfamiliar words mean.	☐ Do Activity 6, p. 193.
	☐ For additional practice, do Activities 1–2, p. 55 in the **Grammatikheft** and Activities 2–3, p. 74 in the **Übungsheft**.
	☐ For interactive practice, do Activity 1, Chapter 7, Disc 2 of the **Interactive CD-ROM Tutor**.
Study the **So sagt man das!** box on p. 194: Extending and responding to an invitation. You should know how to invite someone to go somewhere and how to accept or decline an invitation.	☐ Do Activity 9, p. 195 as a writing activity. Write an imaginary conversation between yourself and a friend. Do not yet give reasons why an invitation has to be declined.
Study the **So sagt man das!** box on p. 194: Expressing obligations. You should now be able to explain why you are declining an invitation.	☐ Complete Activity 9, p. 195 by supplying a reason each time an invitation is declined.
	☐ For additional practice, do Activity 10, p. 195.
Study the **Grammatik** box on p. 195: The verb **müssen**. Learn the forms of **müssen**.	☐ Do Activity 12, p. 195 and then do Activity 14, p. 196 as a writing activity.
	☐ For additional practice, do Activities 1–2, p. 208, **Mehr Grammatikübungen**.
	☐ For more practice, do Activities 3–4, p. 56 in the **Grammatikheft** and Activities 4–8, pp. 75–76 in the **Übungsheft**.
	☐ For interactive practice, do Activity 2, Chapter 7, Disc 2 of the **Interactive CD-ROM Tutor**.
Look at the **Ein wenig Grammatik (Schon bekannt)** box on p. 196. This box covers material you learned in Chapter 5.	☐ If any of the information presented here looks unfamiliar to you, review the **Grammatik** box on p. 143.
	☐ Do Activity 16, p. 196.
	☐ For additional practice, do Activity 3, p. 208, **Mehr Grammatikübungen**.
	☐ For more practice, do Activities 5–6, p. 57 in the **Grammatikheft**.

German 1 Komm mit!, Chapter 7

Name _____ Klasse _____ Datum _____

■ Erste Stufe Self-Test

Can you extend and respond to an invitation?	How would you invite a friend to go a. to a movie b. to a café c. shopping d. swimming Accept or decline the following invitations. If you decline, give a reason why you can't go. a. Wir gehen jetzt in eine Disko. Komm doch mit! b. Ich muss in die Stadt gehen. Möchtest du mitkommen? c. Wir spielen jetzt Tennis. Kannst du mitkommen?
Can you express obligation using **müssen**?	Say that the people below have to do the things indicated. a. Bernd, mow the lawn b. Leyla, water the flowers c. Pedro und Felipe, set the table d. Karin, clean up her room

For an online self-test, go to go.hrw.com

WK3 MUENCHEN-7

KAPITEL 7

Name _____ Klasse _____ Datum _____

Zu Hause helfen

■ Zweite Stufe Student Make-Up Assignments Checklist
Pupil's Edition, pp. 198–201

Study the **So sagt man das!** box on p. 198: Talking about how often you have to do things. You should now be able to tell someone how frequently you carry out certain tasks.	☐ Do Activities 9–10, p. 77 in the **Übungsheft**.
Study the **Wortschatz** on p. 198. Read the words aloud until you can say them easily.	☐ Do Activity 17, p. 198. ☐ For additional practice, do Activities 7–8, p. 58 in the **Grammatikheft**.
Study the **So sagt man das!** box on p. 199: Asking for and offering help, and telling someone what to do. You should be able to ask for and offer assistance with chores.	☐ Do Activity 3, Chapter 7, Disc 2 of the **Interactive CD-ROM Tutor**.
Study the **Ein wenig Grammatik** box on p. 199. You will need to learn the forms of **können**.	☐ Do Activity 19, p. 199 and Activity 20, p. 200. ☐ For additional practice, do Activities 5–7, p. 209, **Mehr Grammatikübungen**. ☐ For more practice, do Activities 9–10, p. 59 in the **Grammatikheft** and Activity 11, p. 77 in the **Übungsheft**.
Study the **Grammatik** box on p. 200: The accusative pronouns. Practice saying the pronouns over and over until you have them memorized.	☐ Do Activities 21 and 23, p. 201. ☐ For additional practice, do Activities 8–9, p. 210, **Mehr Grammatikübungen**. ☐ For more practice, do Activities 11–12, p. 60 in the **Grammatikheft** and Activities 12–14, pp. 78–79 in the **Übungsheft**. ☐ For interactive practice, do Activity 4, Chapter 7, Disc 2 of the **Interactive CD-ROM Tutor**.

German 1 Komm mit!, Chapter 7   Student Make-Up Assignments **41**

Copyright © by Holt, Rinehart and Winston. All rights reserved.

Name _____ Klasse _____ Datum _____

■ Zweite Stufe Self-Test

Can you talk about how often you have to do things?	How would you ask a classmate how often he or she has to
	a. wash the windows
	b. vacuum
	c. clear the table
	d. do the dishes
	How would you tell a classmate how often you have to do each of the things above?

Can you offer help and tell someone what to do using expressions with **für**?	How would you ask a classmate if you could help him or her? How would you ask two classmates?
	Using **können**, explain to each of these people what they can do to help you.
	a. Sara: das Geschirr spülen
	b. Silke und Peter: das Zimmer aufräumen
	c. Markus: das Bett machen
	d. Claudia und Daniel: den Tisch decken
	How might a friend respond if he or she agreed to do some chores for you?

go.hrw.com   For an online self-test, go to go.hrw.com

WK3 MUENCHEN-7

Name _____ Klasse _____ Datum _____

KAPITEL 7 Zu Hause helfen

■ Dritte Stufe Student Make-Up Assignments Checklist
Pupil's Edition, pp. 202–205

Study the **Wortschatz** on p. 202. Try to guess what all the words mean before looking them up.	☐ Do Activity 25, p. 202.
Study the **So sagt man das!** box on p. 203: Talking about the weather. You should be able to ask and tell about weather conditions.	☐ Do Activities 13–14, p. 61 in the **Grammatikheft** and Activities 15–21, pp. 80–82 in the **Übungsheft**. ☐ For interactive practice, do Activities 5–6, Chapter 7, Disc 2 of the **Interactive CD-ROM Tutor**.
Study the **Ein wenig Grammatik** box on p. 203. Use the word **morgen** and some of the chore vocabulary from the **Erste Stufe** to come up with more examples of this grammar point.	☐ Do Activity 27, p. 203 as a writing activity and Activity 28, p. 204. ☐ For additional practice, do Activity 10, p. 211, **Mehr Grammatikübungen**. ☐ For more practice, do Activities 15–16, p. 62 in the **Grammatikheft**.
Study the **Wortschatz** on p. 204. Why do you think the German names for the months are so similar to the English names?	☐ Do Activity 29, p. 205. ☐ For additional practice, do Activities 17–18, p. 63 in the **Grammatikheft**.

German 1 Komm mit!, Chapter 7   Student Make-Up Assignments **43**

Name _____ Klasse _____ Datum _____

■ Dritte Stufe Self-Test

KAPITEL 7

Can you talk about the weather?

How would you tell a classmate what the weather is like today? How would you tell him or her the weather forecast for tomorrow?

How would you tell someone new to your area what the weather is like in

a. January
b. March
c. June
d. October
e. December

go.hrw.com For an online self-test, go to go.hrw.com

WK3 MUENCHEN-7

44 Student Make-Up Assignments   German 1 Komm mit!, Chapter 7

Copyright © by Holt, Rinehart and Winston. All rights reserved.

Name _____ Klasse _____ Datum _____

KAPITEL 8

Einkaufen gehen

■ Erste Stufe Student Make-Up Assignments Checklist
Pupil's Edition, pp. 221–224

Study the **Wortschatz** on p. 221. Read the new vocabulary out loud until you can pronounce all the words fluently. The pictures will help you figure out the meanings of any unfamiliar words.	☐ Do Activity 7, p. 222. ☐ For additional practice, do Activities 1–2, p. 64 in the **Grammatikheft** and Activities 2–4, pp. 86–87 in the **Übungsheft**. ☐ For interactive practice, do Activity 1, Chapter 8, Disc 2 of the **Interactive CD-ROM Tutor**.
Study the **So sagt man das!** box on p. 222: Asking what you should do. You should be able to ask how you can help someone and to ask for advice.	☐ Use the food items you picked out for Activity 7 to write a short conversation. Ask a friend or family member where you should buy each item and he or she responds by telling you which type of store is most likely to carry the item.
Study the **Grammatik** box on p. 223: The verb **sollen**. Learn all the forms of sollen.	☐ Do Activity 9, p. 223. ☐ For additional practice, do Activities 1–2, p. 236, **Mehr Grammatikübungen**. ☐ For more practice, do Activities 3–4, p. 65 in the **Grammatikheft** and Activities 5–6, p. 87 in the **Übungsheft**.
Study the **So sagt man das!** box on p. 223: Telling someone what to do. Try to figure out how the singular and plural command forms, **geh** and **geht**, are derived from the infinitive **gehen**.	☐ Using the shopping list from Activity 10, p. 223, write commands telling someone where to go to find each item. Example: Wurst – Geh (Geht) zur Metzgerei! (Note: **zur** is used before feminine nouns and **zum** before masculine nouns.)
Study the **Grammatik** box on p. 224: The **du**-command and the **ihr**-command. You should now be able to convert the verbs you know into informal command forms.	☐ Do Activity 12, p. 224. ☐ For additional practice, do Activity 4, p. 237, **Mehr Grammatikübungen**. ☐ For more practice, do Activities 5–6, p. 66 in the **Grammatikheft** and Activities 7–8, p. 88 in the **Übungsheft**. ☐ For interactive practice, do Activity 2, Chapter 8, Disc 2 of the **Interactive CD-ROM Tutor**.

German 1 Komm mit!, Chapter 8

Name _____ Klasse _____ Datum _____

■ Erste Stufe Self-Test

Can you ask someone what you should do using **sollen**?	How would you ask someone what you should do for him or her? How might he or she answer using the following items? a. bread: at the baker's b. ground meat: at the butcher's c. milk: at the supermarket d. apples: at the produce store
Can you tell someone what to do using a **du**-command?	How would you tell someone where to buy the food items above? How would you tell a friend to a. mow the lawn b. buy 500 grams of tomatoes c. clean the room d. get 6 apples

For an online self-test, go to go.hrw.com

WK3 MUENCHEN-8

46 Student Make-Up Assignments — German 1 Komm mit!, Chapter 8

Name _____ Klasse _____ Datum _____

KAPITEL 8 Einkaufen gehen

■ Zweite Stufe Student Make-Up Assignments Checklist
Pupil's Edition, pp. 226–228

Study the **Wortschatz** on p. 226. Read the vocabulary out loud, making sure you understand what it means.	☐ Do Activties 7–8, p. 67 in the **Grammatikheft**. ☐ For additional practice, do Activities 9–10, pp. 89–90 in the **Übungsheft**.
Study the **So sagt man das!** box on p. 226: Talking about quantities. You should be able to ask how much of an item someone wants and to answer such a question.	☐ Do Activity 15, p. 227 as a writing activity. Write out a conversation between yourself and a salesperson.
Study the **So sagt man das!** box on p. 227: Saying that you want something else. You should be able to ask someone if they want something else and to respond to such a question.	☐ Do Activity 17, p. 228 as a writing activity. Pick one of the recipes shown and write a conversation between yourself and a salesperson. The salesperson should ask you what you need, how much of it you need and whether or not you need anything else. ☐ For more practice, do Activities 9–11, p. 68 in the **Grammatikheft** and Activities 11–14, pp. 90–91 in the **Übungsheft**. ☐ For interactive practice, do Activity 3, Chapter 8, Disc 2 of the **Interactive CD-ROM Tutor**.

German 1 Komm mit!, Chapter 8 Student Make-Up Assignments **47**

Name _____ Klasse _____ Datum _____

■ Zweite Stufe Self-Test

Can you ask for specific quantities?	How would you tell a salesperson you need the following things? a. 500 Gramm Hackfleisch b. Brot c. 1 Liter Milch d. 1 Pfd. Tomaten e. 2 Kilo Kartoffeln
Can you say that you want something else?	How would a salesperson ask you if you wanted something else? How would you respond using the following items? a. 10 Semmeln b. 100 Gramm Aufschnitt c. 200 Gramm Käse

For an online self-test, go to go.hrw.com

WK3 MUENCHEN-8

48 Student Make-Up Assignments

German 1 Komm mit!, Chapter 8

Name _____ Klasse _____ Datum _____

KAPITEL 8 Einkaufen gehen

■ Dritte Stufe Student Make-Up Assignments Checklist
Pupil's Edition, pp. 229–233

Study the **So sagt man das!** box on p. 230: Giving reasons. You should be able to explain why you do something, using **weil** or **denn**.	☐ Look back at the chore vocabulary in Chapter 7, p. 193. Using **weil** and **denn**, write out five reasons why you cannot go out with your friends today.
Study the **Ein wenig Grammatik** box on p. 230. How does word order change depending on whether you use **denn** or **weil**?	☐ Do Activity 22, p. 230 and Activity 23, p. 231. ☐ For additional practice, do Activity 8, p. 238, **Mehr Grammatikübungen**. ☐ For more practice, do Activities 12–13, p. 69 in the **Grammatikheft** and Activities 15–19, pp. 92–93 in the **Übungsheft**. ☐ For interactive practice, do Activity 4, Chapter 8, Disc 2 of the **Interactive CD-ROM Tutor**.
Study the **So sagt man das!** box on p. 231: Saying where you were and what you bought. Pay close attention to how the past-tense verbs are formed.	☐ Do Activities 14–15, p. 70 in the **Grammatikheft**. ☐ For interactive practice, do Activity 6, Chapter 8, Disc 2, on the **Interactive CD-ROM Tutor**.
Study the **Wortschatz** on p. 231. Read the words aloud until you can pronounce each one fluently.	☐ Using the text in the **So sagt man das!** box on p. 231 as a model, write a sentence using each of the new vocabulary terms. Write about where you were or what you were doing at each of the times listed.
Study the **Grammatik** box on p. 231: The past tense of sein. Learn these verb forms.	☐ Do Activity 25, p. 232 as a writing activity and then do Activity 26, p. 232. ☐ For additional practice, do Activities 9–10, p. 239, **Mehr Grammatikübungen**. ☐ For more practice, do Activities 16–18, pp. 71–72 in the **Grammatikheft** and Activities 20–22, p. 94 in the **Übungsheft**. ☐ For interactive practice, do Activity 5, Chapter 8, Disc 2 of the **Interactive CD-ROM Tutor**.

German 1 Komm mit!, Chapter 8   Student Make-Up Assignments **49**

Name _____ Klasse _____ Datum _____

■ Dritte Stufe Self-Test

Can you give reasons using **denn** and **weil**?	How would you say that you can't do each of the following and give a reason why not? a. go to a movie b. go shopping c. go to a café
Can you say where you were (using **sein**) and what you bought?	How would you ask someone where he or she was yesterday? How would you ask two friends? Can you say where you were using the following cues? a. at the baker's in the morning b. at the supermarket yesterday c. at the butcher's yesterday morning d. at home this afternoon How would you ask your friend what he or she bought? How would you say that you bought the following items? a. bread b. a shirt c. a sweater d. cheese e. pants

KAPITEL 8

go.hrw.com   For an online self-test, go to go.hrw.com

WK3 MUENCHEN-8

50   Student Make-Up Assignments   German 1 Komm mit!, Chapter 8

Copyright © by Holt, Rinehart and Winston. All rights reserved.

Name _____ Klasse _____ Datum _____

KAPITEL 9 Amerikaner in München

■ Erste Stufe Student Make-Up Assignments Checklist
Pupil's Edition, pp. 249–251

Study the **Wortschatz** on p. 249. Can you guess what the words mean, based on their corresponding illustrations?	☐ Do Activities 1–2, p. 73 in the **Grammatikheft**. ☐ For additional practice, do Activities 2–3, p. 98 in the **Übungsheft**. ☐ For interactive practice, do Activity 1, Chapter 9, Disc 3 of the **Interactive CD-ROM Tutor**.
Study the **So sagt man das!** box on p. 250: Talking about where something is located. You should know how to ask where something is and how to respond to such a question.	☐ Do Activities 5–6, p. 75 in the **Grammatikheft**.
Study the **Grammatik** box on p. 250: The verb **wissen**. Learn these verb forms.	☐ Do Activities 7–8, p. 251. ☐ For additional practice, do Activity 1, p. 264, **Mehr Grammatikübungen**. ☐ For more practice, do Activities 3–4, p. 74 in the **Grammatikheft** and Activities 4–8, pp. 99–100 in the **Übungsheft**. ☐ For interactive practice, do Activity 2, Chapter 9, Disc 3 of the **Interactive CD-ROM Tutor**.

Name _____ Klasse _____ Datum _____

■ Erste Stufe Self-Test

| Can you talk about where something is located? | How would you ask an older passerby where the following places are using **wissen**? How would you ask someone who is your own age? How would you answer?
a. Frauenkirche (… Straße)
b. Rathaus (Marienplatz)
c. Museum (Maximilianstraße) |

go.hrw.com For an online self-test, go to go.hrw.com

WK3 MUENCHEN-9

KAPITEL 9

52 Student Make-Up Assignments   German 1 Komm mit!, Chapter 9

KAPITEL 9 — Amerikaner in München

Name _____ Klasse _____ Datum _____

■ Zweite Stufe Student Make-Up Assignments Checklist
Pupil's Edition, pp. 253–256

Study the **Wortschatz** on p. 253. Read the sentences aloud and make sure you understand what they mean.	☐ Do Activity 13, p. 254. ☐ For additional practice, do Activities 7–10, pp. 76–77 in the **Grammatikheft**.
Study the **So sagt man das!** box on p. 254: Asking for and giving directions. Make note of the different ways you can ask for directions and the multiple forms your answer can take.	☐ Do Activity 14, p. 255 as a writing activity. Write out a conversation between yourself and a friend. Each of you should ask the other for directions to two different places. ☐ For additional practice, do Activity 17, p. 256. ☐ For more practice, do Activities 9–11, pp. 101–102 in the **Übungsheft**. ☐ For interactive practice, do Activity 3, Chapter 9, Disc 3 of the **Interactive CD-ROM Tutor**.
Study the **Ein wenig Grammatik** box on p. 255. You should know when to use **fahren** and when to use **gehen** when giving directions.	☐ For additional practice with the verb **fahren** do Activity 4, p. 265, **Mehr Grammatikübungen**. ☐ For additional practice, do Activities 12–13, p. 102 in the **Übungsheft**.
Study the **Grammatik** box on p. 255: The formal commands with **Sie**. You should know how to express formal commands and when to use them.	☐ Do Activity 18, p. 256 as a writing activity. Play the role of the German student and give formal directions to the two tourists who come to you for information. ☐ For additional practice, do Activity 6, p. 266, **Mehr Grammatikübungen**. ☐ For more practice, do Activities 11–12, p. 78 in the **Grammatikheft** and Activities 14–15, p. 103 in the **Übungsheft**. ☐ For interactive practice, do Activity 4, Chapter 9, Disc 3 of the **Interactive CD-ROM Tutor**.

German 1 Komm mit!, Chapter 9

Zweite Stufe Self-Test

Can you ask for and give directions?

Look at the map on p. 270 in your book. How would you ask for directions from the **X**-mark to the following places?

a. Bahnhof
b. Theater
c. Marktplatz
d. Bank

How would you tell an older person to get to the following places using the command forms? Someone your own age? Use the **X**-mark as the starting point.

By vehicle:
a. to the train station
b. to the town hall

On foot:
a. to the supermarket
b. to the café

For an online self-test, go to go.hrw.com

WK3 MUENCHEN-9

KAPITEL 9 — Amerikaner in München

Name _____ Klasse _____ Datum _____

■ Dritte Stufe Student Make-Up Assignments Checklist
Pupil's Edition, pp. 257–261

Study the **So sagt man das!** box on p. 257: Talking about what there is to eat and drink. You should be able to ask and tell someone what is available.	☐ Do Activities 16–17, p. 104 in the **Übungsheft**.
Study the **Ein wenig Grammatik** box on p. 257. Know how to use **es gibt** in both questions and statements.	☐ Do Activity 20, p. 257 as a writing activity. Write a conversation between yourself and a friend. ☐ For additional practice, do Activity 7, p. 266, **Mehr Grammatikübungen**. ☐ For more practice, do Activities 13–14, p. 79 in the **Grammatikheft**.
Study the **So sagt man das!** box on p. 258: Saying you do or don't want more. Read the questions and statements aloud, noting the various ways in which you can tell someone that you do or do not want more to eat or drink.	☐ Do Activity 22, p. 258. ☐ For additional practice, do Activity 15, p. 80 in the **Grammatikheft** and Activity 18, p. 105 in the **Übungsheft**.
Look at the **Ein wenig Grammatik (Schon bekannt)** box on p. 258. This box covers material you learned in Chapter 5.	☐ If any of the information presented here looks unfamiliar to you, review the **Grammatik** box on p. 135. ☐ For additional practice with **noch + ein**, do Activity 8, p. 266, **Mehr Grammatikübungen**. ☐ For additional practice, do Activity 19, p. 105 in the **Übungsheft**.
Study the **Grammatik** box on p. 259: Negation of indefinite articles with **kein**. You should know when and how to use **kein** in a sentence.	☐ Do Activity 23, p. 259 as a writing activity and then do Activity 24, p. 259. ☐ For additional practice, do Activity 9, p. 267, **Mehr Grammatikübungen**. ☐ For more practice, do Activities 16–17, p. 80 in the **Grammatikheft** and Activity 20, p. 105 in the **Übungsheft**. ☐ For interactive practice, do Activity 5, Chapter 9, Disc 3 of the **Interactive CD-ROM Tutor**.

German 1 Komm mit!, Chapter 9   Student Make-Up Assignments **55**

Name _____ Klasse _____ Datum _____

Study the **So sagt man das!** box on p. 260: Expressing opinions. You should know how to use **dass**-clauses in statements of opinion.	☐ Do Activity 26, p. 260.
Study the **Grammatik** box on p. 260: The conjunction **dass**. Note how use of the word **dass** affects word order.	☐ Do Activities 28–29, p. 261. ☐ For additional practice, do Activity 10, p. 267, **Mehr Grammatikübungen**. ☐ For more practice, do Activities 18–19, p. 81 in the **Grammatikheft** and Activities 21–22, p. 106 in the **Übungsheft**. ☐ For interactive practice, do Activity 6, Chapter 9, Disc 3 of the **Interactive CD-ROM Tutor**.

■ Dritte Stufe Self-Test

Can you talk about what there is to eat and drink?	How would you ask what there is to eat? And to drink? How would you tell someone what there is to eat or drink, using the items below? a. **Leberkäs** d. tea b. whole wheat rolls e. salad c. apple juice f. grilled chicken
Can you ask or tell someone that you do or don't want more?	How would you ask someone if he or she wants more? How would you tell someone that you want more of the items below or that you don't want more, using **noch ein** and **kein … mehr**? a. a piece of cake c. mineral water b. roll d. ice cream
Can you express opinions using **dass**-clauses?	How would you give your opinion about the following statement? How would you agree with it? And disagree? **Autofahren ist gefährlich.** State your opinions about school in general. Write at least two sentences using **dass**-clauses.

For an online self-test, go to go.hrw.com

WK3 MUENCHEN-9

Name _____ Klasse _____ Datum _____

KAPITEL 10 Kino und Konzerte

■ Erste Stufe Student Make-Up Assignments Checklist
Pupil's Edition, pp. 281–284

Study the **Wortschatz** on p. 281. Read the new vocabulary out loud and make sure you understand what it means.	☐ Do Activity 6, p. 282. ☐ For additional practice, do Activity 1, p. 82 in the **Grammatikheft**. ☐ For interactive practice, do Activity 1, Chapter 10, Disc 3 of the **Interactive CD-ROM Tutor**.
Study the **So sagt man das!** box on p. 282: Expressing likes and dislikes. You know how to ask someone what he or she likes or dislikes and how to answer such a question.	☐ Do Activity 2, p. 82 in the **Grammatikheft**. ☐ For additional practice, do Activities 2–4, pp. 110–111 in the **Übungsheft**.
Study the **Wortschatz** on p. 282. Why is the list of words arranged the way it is?	☐ Do Activity 8, p. 282 as a writing activity. Write down ten questions you could ask your classmates.
Study the **Grammatik** box on p. 282: The verb **mögen**. You must learn these verb forms.	☐ Do Activity 9, p. 283 as a writing activity. Write a conversation between yourself and a friend in which you discuss your likes and dislikes. ☐ For additional practice, do Activities 1–2, p. 296, **Mehr Grammatikübungen**. ☐ For more practice, do Activity 3, p. 83 in the **Grammatikheft** and Activities 5–8, pp. 111–112 in the **Übungsheft**. ☐ For interactive practice, do Activity 2, Chapter 10, Disc 3 of the **Interactive CD-ROM Tutor**.
Study the **Wortschatz** on p. 283. Why do you think these German words are so similar to the English terms?	☐ Do Activity 4, p. 83 in the **Grammatikheft**.
Study the **Wortschatz** on p. 284. Read the words aloud and make sure you understand what they mean.	☐ Do Activity 10, p. 284 as a writing activity. Make a chart like the one shown and then fill it out using answers given to you by an imaginary classmate. Use those answers to write the report in part b. ☐ For additional practice, do Activity 5, p. 84 in the **Grammatikheft**.

German 1 Komm mit!, Chapter 10   Student Make-Up Assignments **57**

Name _____ Klasse _____ Datum _____

KAPITEL 10

Study the **So sagt man das!** box on p. 284: Expressing familiarity. You should know how to ask someone if he or she is familiar with something and how to respond to such a question.	☐ Do Activity 12, p. 284 as a writing activity. Write a conversation between two classmates.
Look at the **Ein wenig Grammatik (Schon bekannt)** box on p. 284. This box covers material you learned in Chapter 9.	☐ If any of the information presented here looks unfamiliar to you, review the **Grammatik** box on p. 250. ☐ Do Activity 4, p. 297, **Mehr Grammatikübungen**. ☐ For additional practice, do Activity 6, p. 84 in the **Grammatikheft**.

■ Erste Stufe Self-Test

Can you express likes and dislikes using **mögen**?	How would you ask a friend what type of movie he or she likes? How might he or she respond? How would you say that a. Thomas likes horror films a lot b. Julia really doesn't like rock music at all c. Sabine and Nicole like fantasy films d. We don't care for romance movies
Can you express familiarity using **kennen**?	How would a friend ask if you are familiar with a. the movie *Air Force One* b. the singer Ina Deter c. the group R.E.M. d. the film star Clint Eastwood How would you respond to each of your friend's questions?

go.hrw.com For an online self-test, go to go.hrw.com

WK3 BADEN-WUERTTEMBERG-10

58 Student Make-Up Assignments German 1 Komm mit!, Chapter 10

Copyright © by Holt, Rinehart and Winston. All rights reserved.

Name _____ Klasse _____ Datum _____

KAPITEL 10 Kino und Konzerte

■ Zweite Stufe Student Make-Up Assignments Checklist
Pupil's Edition, pp. 285–288

Study the **So sagt man das!** box on p. 285: Expressing preferences and favorites. Know how to ask someone about his or her preferences and favorites and how to respond to such questions.	☐ Do Activity 3, Chapter 10, Disc 3 of the **Interactive CD-ROM Tutor.**
Study the first **Ein wenig Grammatik** box on p. 285. Know how to use **lieber** and **am liebsten** in a sentence.	☐ Do Activity 5, p. 297, **Mehr Grammatikübungen.** ☐ For additional practice, do Activity 7, p. 85 in the **Grammatikheft.**
Study the second **Ein wenig Grammatik** box on p. 285. You might want to create a chart showing the different forms of **sehen**.	☐ Do Activity 14, p. 286 as a writing activity. Write a conversation between yourself and a friend. ☐ For additional practice, do Activity 15, p. 286 as a writing activity. Answer the three questions with your own opinions. ☐ For more practice, do Activities 8–9, p. 86 in the **Grammatikheft.**
Study the **Wortschatz** on p. 288. Read the adjectives out loud until you can pronounce them fluently and make sure you understand what they mean.	☐ Do Activity 18, p. 288 as a writing activity. Write a conversation between yourself and a classmate. ☐ For additional practice, do Activities 10–11, p. 87 in the **Grammatikheft** and Activities 9–15, pp. 113–115 in the **Übungsheft.** ☐ For interactive practice, do Activity 4, Chapter 10, Disc 3 of the **Interactive CD-ROM Tutor.**

German 1 Komm mit!, Chapter 10 Student Make-Up Assignments **59**

Name _____ Klasse _____ Datum _____

■ Zweite Stufe Self-Test

| Can you express preferences and favorites? | How would you tell a friend what type of movies you like to see, what type of movies you prefer and what type of movies you like best of all? |

How would you say that

a. Martin likes adventure movies, but prefers movies about romance.

b. Sandra likes horror films best of all.

c. Sabine doesn't like to read magazines (**Zeitschriften**) and prefers to read newspapers (**Zeitungen**).

For an online self-test, go to go.hrw.com

WK3 BADEN-WUERTTEMBERG-10

KAPITEL 10 — Kino und Konzerte

■ Dritte Stufe Student Make-Up Assignments Checklist
Pupil's Edition, pp. 290–293

Study the **Wortschatz** on p. 291. Can you identify the types of books shown in the box, using the new vocabulary?	☐ Do Activity 22, p. 291, parts 1–3. ☐ For additional practice, do Activities 12–14, p. 88 in the **Grammatikheft** and Activities 16–18, pp. 116–117 in the **Übungsheft**. ☐ For interactive practice, do Activity 5, Chapter 10, Disc 3 of the **Interactive CD-ROM Tutor**.
Study the **Grammatik** box on p. 291: Stem-changing verbs. You will need to learn the present-tense forms of **lesen** and **sprechen**. You should know how to use **sprechen über** and **worüber** in a sentence.	☐ Do Activity 22, p. 291, part 4. ☐ Do Activity 23, p. 292 and then do Activity 24, p. 292 as a writing activity. Write out a conversation between a salesperson and a customer in a bookstore. ☐ For practice, do Activity 7, p. 299, **Mehr Grammatikübungen**. ☐ For additional practice, do Activities 15–16, p. 89 in the **Grammatikheft**. ☐ For more practice, do Activities 19–20, p. 117 in the **Übungsheft**. ☐ For interactive practice, do Activity 6, Chapter 10, Disc 3, on the **Interactive CD-ROM Tutor**.
Study the **So sagt man das!** box on p. 292: Talking about what you did in your free time. Take note of the sequencing words used, as well as the forms of the verbs.	☐ Do Activities 27 and 29, p. 293. ☐ For additional practice, do Activity 8, p. 299, **Mehr Grammatikübungen**. ☐ For more practice, do Activities 17–19, p. 90 in the **Grammatikheft** and Activities 21–22, p. 118 in the **Übungsheft**.

German 1 Komm mit!, Chapter 10   Student Make-Up Assignments **61**

Name _____ Klasse _____ Datum _____

■ Dritte Stufe Self-Test

KAPITEL 10

Can you talk about what you did in your free time?	How would you ask a friend what he or she did on the weekend? How would your friend respond if he or she

a. saw the movie *The Lost World* on Saturday evening

b. read a newspaper on Sunday

c. saw the movie *Michael Collins* on video on Friday evening

d. read the book *The Horse Whisperer* on Saturday

e. was at the Billy Joel concert on Friday evening

f. bought clothes and talked about fashion with his or her friends

Write a short paragraph describing what you saw, read, or talked about with your friends last weekend.

go.hrw.com For an online self-test, go to go.hrw.com

WK3 BADEN-WUERTTEMBERG-10

KAPITEL 11 — Der Geburtstag

Name _____ Klasse _____ Datum _____

■ Erste Stufe Student Make-Up Assignments Checklist
Pupil's Edition, pp. 309–312

Study the **Wortschatz** on p. 309. Read the words and sentences out loud and make sure you understand what they mean.	☐ Do Activity 6, p. 309. ☐ For additional practice, do Activities 1–2, pp. 91–92 in the **Grammatikheft**. ☐ For interactive practice, do Activity 1, Chapter 11, Disc 3, of the **Interactive CD-ROM Tutor**.
Study the **So sagt man das!** box on p. 310: Using the telephone in Germany. You should know the standard phrases used when carrying on a telephone conversation.	☐ Do Activity 8, p. 310 and Activity 9, p. 311 as writing activities. ☐ For additional practice, do Activity 1, p. 324, **Mehr Grammatikübungen**. ☐ For more practice, do Activity 3, p. 92 in the **Grammatikheft** and Activities 2–7, pp. 122–124 in the **Übungsheft**.

German 1 Komm mit!, Chapter 11   Student Make-Up Assignments

Name _____ Klasse _____ Datum _____

■ Erste Stufe Self-Test

| Can you use the telephone in Germany? |

If you were calling someone in Germany, how would you

a. say who you are

b. ask to speak to someone

c. say hello to the person you want to speak with

d. say goodbye

If you were answering the phone in Germany, how would you

a. identify yourself

b. ask the caller to wait a minute

How would you tell someone how to use a public telephone to make a call? (Use **zuerst, dann, danach** and **zuletzt**.)

For an online self-test, go to go.hrw.com

WK3 BADEN-WUERTTEMBERG-11

KAPITEL 11 — Der Geburtstag

Name _____ Klasse _____ Datum _____

Zweite Stufe Student Make-Up Assignments Checklist
Pupil's Edition, pp. 313–315

Study the **So sagt man das!** box on p. 313: Inviting someone to a party and accepting or declining. Read the questions and statements out loud and practice giving a few reasons for declining an invitation.	☐ Do Activities 15–16, p. 313. ☐ For additional practice, do Activity 4, p. 93 in the **Grammatikheft**.
Study the **So sagt man das!** box on p. 314: Talking about birthdays and expressing good wishes. Be able to ask about the date of someone's birthday and to answer such a question. You should also be able to wish someone well on his or her birthday.	☐ Do Activity 3, p. 325, **Mehr Grammatikübungen**. ☐ For additional practice, do Activities 5–6, p. 94 in the **Grammatikheft**. ☐ For interactive practice, do Activity 2, Chapter 11, Disc 3 of the **Interactive CD-ROM Tutor**.
Study the **Wortschatz** on p. 314. What day of the month is your birthday? How would you express that in German?	☐ Do Activity 20, p. 314. ☐ For additional practice, do Activities 7–8, p. 95 in the **Grammatikheft**.
Study the **Wortschatz** on p. 315. Practice reading the new vocabulary aloud.	☐ Do Activities 9–15, pp. 126–127 in the **Übungsheft**. ☐ For interactive practice, do Activity 3, Chapter 11, Disc 3 of the **Interactive CD-ROM Tutor**.

German 1 Komm mit!, Chapter 11   Student Make-Up Assignments **65**

Copyright © by Holt, Rinehart and Winston. All rights reserved.

Name _____ Klasse _____ Datum _____

■ Zweite Stufe Self-Test

Can you invite someone to a party and accept or decline?	How would a friend invite you to his or her birthday party on Saturday evening at 8:00?
	How would you respond if a. you can come b. you can't come because a relative is coming to visit c. you can't come because you are going to a concert d. you can't come because you have to do your homework
Can you talk about birthdays and express good wishes?	How would you ask a friend when he or she has a birthday? How would your friend respond if he or she has a birthday on a. May 29 b. March 9 c. February 16 d. July 7 How would you express good wishes for the following occasions? a. birthday b. Christmas c. Hanukkah

KAPITEL 11

For an online self-test, go to go.hrw.com

WK3 BADEN-WUERTTEMBERG-11

Name _____ Klasse _____ Datum _____

KAPITEL 11 — Der Geburtstag

■ Dritte Stufe Student Make-Up Assignments Checklist
Pupil's Edition, pp. 317–321

Study the **Wortschatz** on p. 317. Read the new vocabulary aloud and make sure you understand the meaning of all of the words.	☐ Do Activity 23, p. 317. ☐ For additional practice, do Activity 9, p. 96 in the **Grammatikheft**. ☐ For interactive practice, do Activity 4, Chapter 11, Disc 3 of the **Interactive CD-ROM Tutor**.
Study the **So sagt man das!** box on p. 318: Discussing gift ideas. Be able to ask someone about his or her gift ideas and to tell someone about your own.	☐ Do Activity 24, p. 318. ☐ For additional practice, do Activity 10, p. 96 in the **Grammatikheft**. ☐ For more practice, do Activities 16–18, pp. 128–129 in the **Übungsheft**.
Study the **Grammatik** box on p. 319: Introduction to the dative case. Create the chart suggested at the bottom of the box and make note of the patterns that are revealed.	☐ Do Activities 3–6, pp. 325–326, **Mehr Grammatikübungen**. ☐ For additional practice, do Activities 11–14, pp. 97–98 in the **Grammatikheft**. ☐ For more practice, do Activities 19–22, pp. 129–130 in the **Übungsheft**. ☐ For interactive practice, do Activity 5, Chapter 11, Disc 3 of the **Interactive CD-ROM Tutor**.
Study the **Grammatik** box on p. 320. You need to know where to place an indirect object in a sentence.	☐ Do Activity 27, p. 320 and then do Activity 28, p. 320 as a writing activity. For Activity 28, write a single sentence for each illustration, telling what gift you are giving to each family member. ☐ For additional practice, do Activities 7–8, p. 326, **Mehr Grammatikübungen**. ☐ For more practice, do Activity 15, p. 99 in the **Grammatikheft**. ☐ For interactive practice, do Activity 6, Chapter 11, Disc 3 of the **Interactive CD-ROM Tutor**.

German 1 Komm mit!, Chapter 11

Name _____ Klasse _____ Datum _____

■ Dritte Stufe Self-Test

Can you discuss gift ideas?	How would you ask a friend what he or she is getting another friend for his or her birthday? How might your friend respond?

How would you tell a friend that you are going to give these items to various relatives for their birthdays?

a. a wristwatch, **mein Vater**
b. perfume, **meine Tante**
c. fancy chocolate, **meine Oma**
d. a poster, **mein Bruder**

For an online self-test, go to go.hrw.com

WK3 BADEN-WUERTTEMBERG-11

KAPITEL 12 — Die Fete

Erste Stufe Student Make-Up Assignments Checklist
Pupil's Edition, pp. 337–340

Look at the **So sagt man das! (Schon bekannt)** box on p. 337: Offering help and explaining what to do. This box covers material you learned in Chapter 7.	☐ If any of the information presented here looks unfamiliar to you, review the **So sagt man das!** box on p. 199. ☐ Do Activities 2–7, pp. 134–136 in the **Übungsheft**.
Look at the **Ein wenig Grammatik (Schon bekannt)** box on p. 337. This box covers material you learned in Chapters 7 and 8.	☐ If any of the information presented here looks unfamiliar to you, review the **Grammatik** boxes on pp. 199, 200 and 224. ☐ Do Activity 6, p. 337 as a writing activity. For part b, write a conversation between yourself and a friend. ☐ For additional practice, do Activities 1–2, p. 352, **Mehr Grammatikübungen**. ☐ For more practice, do Activities 1–3, pp. 100–101 in the **Grammatikheft**.
Study the **Wortschatz** on p. 338. Read the words aloud and make sure you understand what they mean.	☐ Do Activity 7, p. 338 as a writing activity. Pick one of the recipes shown and write a conversation in which you ask a friend to help you by buying the necessary ingredients.
Look at the **So sagt man das! (Schon bekannt)** box on p. 339: Asking where something is located and giving directions. This box covers material you learned in Chapter 9.	☐ If any of the information presented here looks unfamiliar to you, review the **So sagt man das!** boxes on pp. 250 and 254. ☐ Do Activity 10, p. 340 as a writing activity. ☐ For interactive practice, do Activity 1, Chapter 12, Disc 3 of the **Interactive CD-ROM Tutor**.
Look at the **Ein wenig Grammatik (Schon bekannt)** box on p. 340. This box covers material you learned in Chapter 9.	☐ If any of the information presented here looks unfamiliar to you, review the **Grammatik** boxes on pp. 250 and 255. ☐ Do Activities 3–4, p. 353, **Mehr Grammatikübungen**. ☐ For additional practice, do Activities 4–5, p. 102 in the **Grammatikheft**. ☐ For more practice, do Activity 8, p. 136 in the **Übungsheft**.

German 1 Komm mit!, Chapter 12

Name _____ Klasse _____ Datum _____

■ Erste Stufe Self-Test

Can you offer help and explain what to do?	How would you offer to help a classmate do some chores around the house?
	How would he or she respond if he or she needed you to
	a. pick up clothes
	b. clean the windows
	c. go to the store
	d. buy some tomatoes
Can you ask directions and say where something is located?	How would you tell a classmate how to get to school from your house? How would you tell him or her where your school is located?

For an online self-test, go to go.hrw.com

WK3 BADEN-WUERTTEMBERG-12

KAPITEL 12

70 Student Make-Up Assignments

German 1 Komm mit!, Chapter 12

Copyright © by Holt, Rinehart and Winston. All rights reserved.

KAPITEL 12 Die Fete

Name _____ Klasse _____ Datum _____

■ Zweite Stufe Student Make-Up Assignments Checklist
Pupil's Edition, pp. 342–345

Look at the **So sagt man das! (Schon bekannt)** box on p. 342: Making plans and inviting someone to come along. This box covers material you learned in Chapters 7 and 8.	☐ If any of the information presented here looks unfamiliar to you, review the **So sagt man das!** boxes on pp. 194 and 230. ☐ Do Activity 13, p. 343 as a writing activity. Write a conversation between two friends. ☐ For additional practice, do Activities 9–11, p. 137 in the **Übungsheft**.
Study the **Wortschatz** on p. 342. Read the activity vocabulary aloud, making sure you understand all the words.	☐ Do Activity 14b, p. 343 as a writing activity. Write a conversation between yourself and a classmate. ☐ For additional practice, do Activity 7, p. 103 in the **Grammatikheft**. ☐ For interactive practice, do Activity 2, Chapter 12, Disc 3 of the **Interactive CD-ROM Tutor**.
Look at the **Ein wenig Grammatik (Schon bekannt)** box on p. 342. This box covers material you learned in Chapters 6 and 7.	☐ If any of the information presented here looks unfamiliar to you, review the **Grammatik** boxes on pp. 166 and 195. ☐ Do Activity 6, p. 353, **Mehr Grammatikübungen**. ☐ For additional practice, do Activity 6, p. 103 in the **Grammatikheft** and Activity 12, p. 138 in the **Übungsheft**. ☐ For interactive practice, do Activity 3, Chapter 12, Disc 3 of the **Interactive CD-ROM Tutor**.
Look at the **So sagt man das! (Schon bekannt)** box on p. 344: Talking about clothing. This box covers material you learned in Chapter 5.	☐ If any of the information presented here looks unfamiliar to you, review the **So sagt man das!** boxes on pp. 134, 137, 139 and 143. ☐ Do Activities 8–9, p. 104 in the **Grammatikheft**.
Study the **Wortschatz** on p. 344. Practice using the new vocabulary in short sentences.	☐ Do Activity 17, p. 345 as a writing activity. Write a conversation between yourself and a salesperson in a clothing store.

German 1 Komm mit!, Chapter 12   Student Make-Up Assignments

Name _____ Klasse _____ Datum _____

Look at the first **Ein wenig Grammatik (Schon bekannt)** box on p. 345. This box refers you to material you learned in Chapters 5 and 7.	☐ If any of the information presented here looks unfamiliar to you, review the **Grammatik** boxes on pp. 135 and 200. ☐ Do Activity 13, p. 138 in the **Übungsheft**.
Look at the **So sagt man das! (Schon bekannt)** box on p. 345: Discussing gift ideas. This box covers material you learned in Chapter 11.	☐ If any of the information presented here looks unfamiliar to you, review the **So sagt man das!** box on p. 318. ☐ Do Activity 18, p. 345 as a writing activity. Write a conversation between yourself and a friend.
Look at the second **Ein wenig Grammatik (Schon bekannt)** box on p. 345. This box covers material you learned in Chapter 11.	☐ If any of the information presented here looks unfamiliar to you, review the **Grammatik** box on p. 319. ☐ Do Activity 8, p. 354, **Mehr Grammatikübungen**. ☐ For additional practice, do Activities 10–11, p. 105 in the **Grammatikheft** and Activities 14–15, p. 139 in the **Übungsheft**.

■ Zweite Stufe Self-Test

Can you make plans and invite someone to come along?	How would your friend invite you to go to a concert at 8:30 on Saturday evening? How would you respond if a. you accept b. you decline because you're going to a movie at 8:00
Can you talk about clothes in a clothing store?	Write a conversation you would have with a salesperson in a clothing store. Talk about particular items of clothing, price, color, fit and make some comments about how the clothing looks on you.
Can you discuss gift ideas?	How would you tell a classmate what you plan to give two family members for their birthdays?

For an online self-test, go to go.hrw.com

WK3 BADEN-WUERTTEMBERG-12

Name _____ Klasse _____ Datum _____

KAPITEL 12 Die Fete

■ Dritte Stufe Student Make-Up Assignments Checklist
Pupil's Edition, pp. 346–349

Look at the **So sagt man das! (Schon bekannt)** box on p. 346: Describing people and places. This box covers material you learned in Chapters 1, 2 and 3.	☐ If any of the information presented here looks unfamiliar to you, review the **So sagt man das!** boxes on pp. 28, 48, 73, 79, 82 and 84.
	☐ Do Activity 12, p. 106 in the **Grammatikheft**.
	☐ For additional practice, do Activities 16–20, pp. 140–141 in the **Übungsheft**.
Look at the **Ein wenig Grammatik (Schon bekannt)** box on p. 346. This box covers material you learned in Chapters 1 and 3.	☐ If any of the information presented here looks unfamiliar to you, review the **Grammatik** boxes on pp. 26, 82 and 83.
	☐ Do Activity 19, p. 346 as a writing activity. Choose a famous person and describe him or her with enough detail that your classmates could guess his or her identity.
	☐ For additional practice, do Activity 9, p. 354, **Mehr Grammatikübungen**.
	☐ For interactive practice, do Activity 4, Chapter 12, Disc 3 of the **Interactive CD-ROM Tutor**.
Study the **Wortschatz** on p. 347. Try to guess what the words mean before looking them up.	☐ Do Activity 22, p. 347 as a writing activity. Choose one of the rooms shown and describe it in detail. You should include your opinion of the furniture.
	☐ For additional practice, do Activities 13–15, p. 107 in the **Grammatikheft**.
	☐ For interactive practice, do Activity 5, Chapter 12, Disc 3 of the **Interactive CD-ROM Tutor**.
Look at the **So sagt man das! (Schon bekannt)** box on p. 348: Saying what you would like and whether you do or don't want more. This box covers material you learned in Chapters 3 and 8.	☐ If any of the information presented here looks unfamiliar to you, review the **So sagt man das!** boxes on pp. 74 and 227.
	☐ Do Activities 21–23, p. 142 in the **Übungsheft**.
	☐ For interactive practice, do Activity 6, Chapter 12, Disc 3 of the **Interactive CD-ROM Tutor**.

German 1 Komm mit!, Chapter 12   Student Make-Up Assignments **73**

Name _____ Klasse _____ Datum _____

Look at the **Ein wenig Grammatik (Schon bekannt)** box on p. 348. This box covers material you learned in Chapters 3 and 9.	☐ If any of the information presented here looks unfamiliar to you, review the **Grammatik** boxes on pp. 75 and 259.
	☐ Do Activity 24, p. 348 as a writing activity. Write a conversation between yourself and two friends, one of whom is your host.
	☐ For additional practice, do Activity 10, p. 355, **Mehr Grammatikübungen**.
	☐ For yet more practice, do Activities 16–17, p. 108 in the **Grammatikheft**.
Look at the **So sagt man das! (Schon bekannt)** box on p. 349: Talking about what you did. This box covers material you learned in Chapter 10.	☐ If any of the information presented here looks unfamiliar to you, review the **So sagt man das!** box on p. 292.
	☐ Do Activity 26, p. 349 as a writing activity. Write a conversation between two classmates.
	☐ For additional practice, do Activity 18, p. 108 in the **Grammatikheft**.

■ Dritte Stufe Self-Test

Can you describe people and places?	How would you describe your best friend: how he or she looks, his or her interests and where he or she lives?
	How would you describe your living room and your kitchen?
Can you say what you would like and that you do or don't want more?	How would you say that you do or don't want more of the following items?
	a. eine Semmel c. ein Apfelsaft
	b. ein Apfel d. ein Käsebrot
Can you talk about what you did?	How would a friend ask you what you did last weekend? How would you respond telling where you were, what you bought, what movies you saw, or what books you read?

go.hrw.com For an online self-test, go to go.hrw.com

WK3 BADEN-WUERTTEMBERG-12

Quizzes

Name _____ Klasse _____ Datum _____

Wer bist du?

Alternative Quiz 1-1A

■ Erste Stufe

Maximum Score: 35

Grammar and Vocabulary

A. Write appropriate hellos and goodbyes using the cues given. (5 points)

Say goodbye to your German teacher, Frau Zellner.

1. _____

Greet your friend Stephan.

2. _____

Say goodbye to your friends Maria and Markus.

3. _____

Greet your math instructor, Frau Schweitzer.

4. _____

Greet your friend Claudia.

5. _____

SCORE _____

B. Complete the following conversation by filling in the blanks with the appropriate words from the word box. (6 points)

| Wer | Hallo | Ja | heißt | Sie | Grüß |

A: 6. _____ dich, Kornelia!

B: 7. _____, Thomas!

A: Wie 8. _____ das Mädchen da?

B: 9. _____ heißt Ulrike.

A: Und der Junge? 10. _____ ist er? Heißt er Peter?

B: 11. _____, er heißt Peter.

SCORE _____

German 1 Komm mit!, Chapter 1   Student Make-Up Assignments   **77**

Name _____ Klasse _____ Datum _____

Alternative Quiz 1-1A

C. Complete the following sentences with the correct form of the verb **heißen.**
(14 points)

Ich 12. _____ Jutta. Und du, wie 13. _____ du?

Der Junge 14. _____ Benjamin.

15. _____ er Max? — Nein, er 16. _____ Markus.

17. _____ du Sara? — Nein, ich 18. _____ Barbara.

SCORE ☐

D. Write the following questions in German using the English sentences as cues.
(10 points)

Who is that?

19. _____

Her name is Sabine.

20. _____

What is his name?

21. _____

Is his name Ludwig?

22. _____

No, the boy's name is Paul.

23. _____

SCORE ☐

TOTAL SCORE ☐

78   Student Make-Up Assignments   German 1 Komm mit!, Chapter 1

Name _____ Klasse _____ Datum _____

Wer bist du?

Zweite Stufe

Alternative Quiz 1-2A

Maximum Score: 35

Grammar and Vocabulary

A. Write out the following numbers and words. (11 points)

1. 13 _____
2. 9 _____
3. 0 _____
4. 4 _____
5. 17 _____
6. 5 _____
7. 15 _____
8. 11 _____
9. 8 _____
10. capital _____
11. federal state _____

SCORE _____

B. Fill in the following blanks with the correct form of the verb **sein**. (12 points)

Wie alt 12. _____ du?

Wie alt 13. _____ die Monika?

Sie 14. _____ dreizehn.

Du 15. _____ siebzehn, nicht?

Nein, ich 16. _____ sechzehn.

Udo und Hugo, sie 17. _____ auch sechzehn.

SCORE _____

German 1 Komm mit!, Chapter 1 — Student Make-Up Assignments

Name _____ Klasse _____ Datum _____

Alternative Quiz 1-2A

C. Fill in the following blanks. (4 points)

A: Du bist fünfzehn, aber 18. _____ bin schon siebzehn.

19. _____ alt ist Manfred?

B: 20. _____ Mädchen ist fünf. Ist der Junge auch fünf

21. _____ alt?

SCORE ☐

D. Write the following questions in German using the English sentences as cues. (8 points)

Is Manuela already sixteen years old?

22. _____

Are Vivian and Angelika nineteen years old?

23. _____

How old am I? I'm seventeen.

24. _____

Are you also twelve years old?

25. _____

SCORE ☐

TOTAL SCORE ☐

Name _____ Klasse _____ Datum _____

Wer bist du?

Alternative Quiz 1-3A

Maximum Score: 30

Dritte Stufe

Grammar and Vocabulary

A. Complete the following questions and statements by filling in the blanks with the appropriate words from the word box. (10 points)

| ist | komme | neu | Wie | heißt | kommst | heiße | |
| Woher | fünfzehn | | | aus | | alt | kommt |

Woher 1. _____ du? Bist du hier 2. _____ ?

3. _____ alt bist du?

Das Mädchen 4. _____ Monika. Sie ist 5. _____ .

Guten Morgen. Ich 6. _____ Herr Fieser, und bin der Deutschlehrer.

Ich 7. _____ aus Berlin.

Er 8. _____ siebzehn Jahre 9. _____ , und er

10. _____ aus Stuttgart.

SCORE _____

B. Write the following sentences in German. (12 points)

Friedrich and Ulrike come to school by bike.

11. _____

How does she come to school? By car?

12. _____

Do you come to school on foot?

13. _____

I come to school by moped, and Ingrid comes to school by subway.

14. _____

SCORE _____

German 1 Komm mit!, Chapter 1 — Student Make-Up Assignments

Name _____ Klasse _____ Datum _____

Alternative Quiz 1-3A

C. Your friend asks you about the new girl at school. Write a note about her in which you answer the following four questions: 1) What is her name? 2) How old is she? 3) Where is she from? 4) How does she get to school? (8 points)

_____
_____
_____
_____
_____
_____
_____
_____
_____
_____
_____
_____
_____
_____
_____

SCORE ☐

TOTAL SCORE ☐

Name _____ Klasse _____ Datum _____

KAPITEL 2 Spiel und Spaß

Erste Stufe

Alternative Quiz 2-1A

Maximum Score: 30

Grammar and Vocabulary

A. A friend of yours is writing to a pen pal in Austria and has asked you to help him with vocabulary for various activities. He has written you a note to fill out, and has left blanks next to the English words that he needs you to translate. Fill in the blanks below with the appropriate German words. (12 points)

Jens plays the piano **1.** _____ and the guitar

2. _____ . He is also an enthusiastic athlete, and spends much of his

free time playing baseball, volleyball **3.** _____ , and soccer

4. _____ . In the evening he often likes to play cards

5. _____ and chess **6.** _____ .

SCORE _____

B. Fill in the following blanks with the appropriate form of the verb in parentheses. (8 points)

(spielen) **7.** _____ er Flöte?

(machen) Was **8.** _____ du in deiner Freizeit?

(spielen) Was **9.** _____ die Ulrike?

(machen) In meiner Freizeit **10.** _____ ich oft Sport.

(spielen) Ich **11.** _____ auch Tennis.

(machen) Und Michael? Was **12.** _____ er?

(spielen) Ich glaube, er **13.** _____ Basketball.

(machen) **14.** _____ du auch Sport?

SCORE _____

German 1 Komm mit!, Chapter 2   Student Make-Up Assignments **83**

Name _____ Klasse _____ Datum _____

Alternative Quiz 2-1A

C. You're taking a straw poll about your friends' interests. Write the following in German, using the English questions and statements as cues. (10 points)

What does Manuela do?

15. _____

She plays chess.

16. _____

She doesn't play cards.

17. _____

Does Udo do sports?

18. _____

Yes, he plays tennis and soccer.

19. _____

SCORE ☐

TOTAL SCORE ☐

Name _____ Klasse _____ Datum _____

KAPITEL 2 Spiel und Spaß

Zweite Stufe

Alternative Quiz 2-2A

Maximum Score: 35

Grammar and Vocabulary

A. Write questions and statements, using all the words given. Note that you will need to provide the German equivalent of the words in parentheses. (20 points)

ich / (hike) / gern

1. _____

Heike und Gisela / (do crafts) / nicht gern

2. _____

(swim) / ihr / oft?

3. _____

ihr / (collect stamps) / gern

4. _____

er / (draw) / nicht gern

5. _____

(visit friends) / sie / gern?

6. _____

du / (listen to music) / sehr gern

7. _____

ich / (dance) / nicht gern

8. _____

(watch TV) / sie (plural) / nicht gern?

9. _____

wir / (hike) / gern

10. _____

SCORE _____

German 1 Komm mit!, Chapter 2   Student Make-Up Assignments   **85**

Name _____ Klasse _____ Datum _____

Alternative Quiz 2-2A

B. Ask the following people a question by filling in the blanks with the correct form of the verb in parentheses, and the correct pronoun. (10 points)

(sammeln) 11. _____ Briefmarken gern, Michael?

(wandern) 12. _____ oft, Heike und Peter?

(schreiben) 13. _____ gern, Herr Böll?

(schwimmen) 14. _____ gern, Werner?

(basteln) 15. _____ gern, Frau Rodler?

SCORE _____

C. Answer the following questions in complete sentences. (5 points)

Was machst du gern?

16. _____

Was machst du nicht so gern?

17. _____

SCORE _____

TOTAL SCORE _____

Name _____ Klasse _____ Datum _____

Spiel und Spaß

Dritte Stufe

Alternative Quiz 2-3A

Maximum Score: 35

Grammar and Vocabulary

A. Match the German word or phrase on the left with its English equivalent on the right. (12 points)

1. _____ im Frühling
2. _____ blöd
3. _____ am Nachmittag
4. _____ interessant
5. _____ am Wochenende
6. _____ Spitze
7. _____ langweilig
8. _____ im Winter
9. _____ im Sommer
10. _____ im Herbst
11. _____ am Abend
12. _____ nach der Schule

a. great
b. in the evening
c. in the summer
d. boring
e. in the winter
f. after school
g. in the afternoon
h. in the spring
i. dumb
j. interesting
k. in the autumn
l. on the weekend

SCORE ____

B. Fill in the following blanks with the appropriate form of the verb in parentheses. (8 points)

(segeln) Im Sommer 13. _____ er.

(tanzen) Ihr 14. _____ jedes Wochenende, nicht?

(finden) Der Udo 15. _____ Zeichnen blöd.

(basteln) Ich 16. _____ nicht so gern.

(sammeln) 17. _____ du gern Briefmarken, Jens?

(wandern) 18. _____ ihr auch im Herbst?

(schwimmen) Nach der Schule 19. _____ ich.

(finden) Wie 20. _____ du Fußball, Heiko?

SCORE ____

German 1 Komm mit!, Chapter 2   Student Make-Up Assignments **87**

Name _____ Klasse _____ Datum _____

Alternative Quiz 2-3A

C. Give the German equivalents of the following sentences. (15 points)

Do you find stamp collecting interesting, Sara?

21. _____

What are you doing after school, Barbara and Inge?

22. _____

In the summer I go hiking.

23. _____

She thinks chess is fantastic. I think so, too.

24. _____

Inge and Peter hike on the weekend.

25. _____

SCORE ☐

TOTAL SCORE ☐

KAPITEL 3 — Komm mit nach Hause!

Alternative Quiz 3-1A
Maximum Score: 35

Erste Stufe

Grammar and Vocabulary

A. Complete the following questions and statements by filling in the blanks with the appropriate words and phrases from the box. (8 points)

| wohnt | mit dem Auto | in der Nähe | wohnen |
| in der Stadt | zu Fuß | ein Vorort von | wohnst |

Sie wohnt weit von hier, und kommt 1. _____ zur Schule.

Das ist der Markus. Er 2. _____ in Starnberg, das ist

3. _____ München.

Wo 4. _____ du? — Ich wohne hier gleich

5. _____ . Ich komme 6. _____ zur Schule.

7. _____ Sie auf dem Land oder 8. _____ ?

SCORE ____

B. Complete each of the following sentences, filling in the first blank with the appropriate form of the verb **möchten,** and the second blank with the equivalent of the words in parentheses. (12 points)

Ich 9. _____ 10. _____ . (a glass of orange juice)

Frau Huber, 11. _____ Sie 12. _____ ? (a piece of cake)

Udo und Heike 13. _____ 14. _____ . (a few cookies)

Ich 15. _____ bitte 16. _____ . (a lemon drink)

17. _____ du jetzt 18. _____ ? (a cola)

Herr Ulrich, 19. _____ Sie 20. _____ ? (fruit)

SCORE ____

German 1 Komm mit!, Chapter 3 — Student Make-Up Assignments 89

Name _____ Klasse _____ Datum _____

Alternative Quiz 3-1A

C. Express the following statements and questions in German. (15 points)

Manfred and Holger, do you live far from here?

21. _____

Yes, we live on Brunnen Street.

22. _____

She would like a few cookies.

23. _____

I would like a glass of apple juice, and he would like a cola.

24. _____

Thank you! — You're welcome!

25. _____

SCORE ☐

TOTAL SCORE ☐

KAPITEL 3

90 Student Make-Up Assignments   German 1 Komm mit!, Chapter 3
Copyright © by Holt, Rinehart and Winston. All rights reserved.

Name _____ Klasse _____ Datum _____

KAPITEL 3
Komm mit nach Hause!

Alternative Quiz 3-2A

Zweite Stufe

Maximum Score: 30

Grammar and Vocabulary

A. For each adjective listed below, write its opposite. (4 points)

1. neu _____
2. hässlich _____
3. unbequem _____
4. klein _____

SCORE ☐

B. For each word listed below, provide the German equivalent. Be sure to include the articles, and put an 'X' next to all plural nouns. (16 points)

5. the chair _____
6. the bookcase _____
7. the bed _____
8. the desk _____
9. the cabinet _____
10. the room _____
11. the stereo _____
12. the furniture _____

SCORE ☐

German 1 Komm mit!, Chapter 3 Student Make-Up Assignments

Name _____ Klasse _____ Datum _____

Alternative Quiz 3-2A

C. Give the German equivalent of the following sentences, using a pronoun in place of the noun in parentheses. (10 points)

(The bed) is uncomfortable.

13. _____

(The couch) is broken.

14. _____

(The furniture) is new.

15. _____

(The chair) is small.

16. _____

(The cabinet) is ugly.

17. _____

SCORE ☐

TOTAL SCORE ☐

Name _____ Klasse _____ Datum _____

KAPITEL 3 Komm mit nach Hause!

Alternative Quiz 3-3A

Maximum Score: 35

Dritte Stufe

Grammar and Vocabulary

A. Write out the following numbers. (10 points)

1. 64 _____
2. 52 _____
3. 27 _____
4. 99 _____
5. 86 _____

6. 44 _____
7. 31 _____
8. 100 _____
9. 25 _____
10. 73 _____

SCORE _____

B. Fill in the following blanks with the correct forms of the possessives **mein, dein,** and **ihr.** (15 points)

Ludwigs Familie ist sehr groß. Das ist Horst, 11. _____ Bruder, und Anna,

12. _____ Schwester. Hier sind 13. _____ Großeltern,

14. _____ Großmutter Frieda und 15. _____ Großvater Heinz.

Der Junge da ist 16. _____ Cousin, und das Mädchen ist

17. _____ Kusine.

A: Hallo, Michael! Ist das 18. _____ Familie?

B: Ja, das sind 19. _____ Eltern, und hier sind 20. _____ Brüder und 21. _____ Onkel.

A: Das ist Heidis Familie. Ist das 22. _____ Bruder?

B: Nein, das ist 23. _____ Cousin Friedrich. Er ist 34 Jahre alt.

A: Hat er auch Haustiere?

B: Ja. Rex ist 24. _____ Hund, und Minka ist 25. _____ Katze.

SCORE _____

German 1 Komm mit!, Chapter 3   Student Make-Up Assignments 93

Name _____ Klasse _____ Datum _____

Alternative Quiz 3-3A

C. Write the following sentences in German. (10 points)

My aunt has long red hair and brown eyes.

26. _____

His mother has short black hair.

27. _____

Your uncle Otto is bald and has glasses, and he is 46 years old.

28. _____

What does her (male) cousin look like?

29. _____

What are the names of Ilse's grandparents?

30. _____

SCORE ☐

TOTAL SCORE ☐

94 Student Make-Up Assignments German 1 Komm mit!, Chapter 3

Name _____ Klasse _____ Datum _____

KAPITEL 4 Alles für die Schule!

Erste Stufe

Alternative Quiz 4-1A

Maximum Score: 35

Grammar and Vocabulary

A. For each word listed below, provide the German equivalent. (9 points)

1. geography _____
2. art _____
3. Tuesday _____
4. history _____
5. Friday _____
6. Saturday _____
7. biology _____
8. chemistry _____
9. Sunday _____

SCORE _____

B. Fill in the following blanks with the appropriate form of the verb **haben**. (10 points)

Jens und Holger, welche Fächer **10.** _____ ihr am Donnerstag? Religion und

Englisch? — Wir **11.** _____ um zehn Uhr Religion, aber Ulrike

12. _____ Sport. Was **13.** _____ Günther?

A: Was **14.** _____ du zuletzt, Gabi?

B: Ich **15.** _____ zuletzt Deutsch.

A: Und Manfred, was **16.** _____ er zuletzt?

B: Ich glaube, er **17.** _____ auch zuletzt Deutsch.

Am Samstag **18.** _____ ich frei. **19.** _____ du auch frei?

SCORE _____

German 1 Komm mit!, Chapter 4   Student Make-Up Assignments **95**

Name _____ Klasse _____ Datum _____

Alternative Quiz 4-1A

C. For each sentence below, provide the German equivalent. Remember to use the sequencing words. (8 points)

I have math first.

20. _____

Then I have chemistry.

21. _____

After that I have geography.

22. _____

Last of all I have physics.

23. _____

SCORE ☐

D. Answer the following questions in complete sentences, according to your own schedule. (8 points)

Wann hast du Englisch?

24. _____

Was hast du um 8 Uhr?

25. _____

Was hast du am Freitag?

26. _____

Welche Fächer hast du am Dienstag?

27. _____

SCORE ☐

TOTAL SCORE ☐

Name _____ Klasse _____ Datum _____

KAPITEL 4
Alles für die Schule!

Zweite Stufe

Alternative Quiz 4-2A
Maximum Score: 30

Grammar and Vocabulary

A. Express each of the following sentences in German. (16 points)

Herr Setzer, do you like soccer?
1. _____

Geography is my favorite subject.
2. _____

Udo and Jens don't like physics.
3. _____

We like art.
4. _____

Manuela and Erika, do you like English?
5. _____

She likes physical education.
6. _____

Peter, is Claudia your favorite cousin?
7. _____

She doesn't like German.
8. _____

SCORE [ ]

B. Respond appropriately to the following statements. (8 points)

Ich habe eine Eins in Mathe.
9. _____

Udo hat eine Zwei in Englisch.
10. _____

German 1 Komm mit!, Chapter 4 — Student Make-Up Assignments

Name _____ Klasse _____ Datum _____

Alternative Quiz 4-2A

Heike hat eine Fünf in Deutsch!

11. _____

Und sie hat auch eine Fünf in Chemie!

12. _____

SCORE [ ]

C. Write in a complete sentence what your friends tell you about their grades, and then react accordingly. (6 points)

Your friend Anna tells you she has an A in geography.

ANNA 13. _____

YOU 14. _____

Your friend Otto tells you that he has failed physics.

OTTO 15. _____

YOU 16. _____

SCORE [ ]

TOTAL SCORE [ ]

Student Make-Up Assignments   German 1 Komm mit!, Chapter 4

Name _____ Klasse _____ Datum _____

4 Alles für die Schule!

Dritte Stufe

Alternative Quiz 4-3A

Maximum Score: 35

Grammar and Vocabulary

A. For each word listed below, provide both the singular and plural German forms. Don't forget to include the articles with each form. (12 points)

1. eraser(s) _____
2. book(s) _____
3. pocket calculator(s) _____
4. dictionary (dictionaries) _____
5. pencil(s) _____
6. school bag(s) _____

SCORE ☐

B. Write the German equivalent of the words and phrases below. (5 points)

7. cheap _____
8. 50 euros _____
9. That's a bargain. _____
10. expensive _____
11. only 3 euros _____

SCORE ☐

German 1 Komm mit!, Chapter 4 — Student Make-Up Assignments

Name _____ Klasse _____ Datum _____

Alternative Quiz 4-3A

C. Complete the following conversation, filling in the blanks with the correct form of **kosten** or the appropriate pronoun. (10 points)

A: Das Heft da. Was 12. _____ 13. _____ ?

B: 14. _____ 15. _____ EUR 1,50.

A: Und wie viel 16. _____ die Kassette?

B: 17. _____ 18. _____ nur 3 Euro.

A: Was 19. _____ die Kulis?

B: 20. _____ 21. _____ bloß EUR 3,30.

SCORE ☐

D. Provide the German equivalent of the following statements and questions. (8 points)

Look! The notebooks are there.

22. _____

The dictionaries are there in the back.

23. _____

The ballpoint pens are here in the front.

24. _____

Are the school supplies over there?

25. _____

SCORE ☐

TOTAL SCORE ☐

100   Student Make-Up Assignments   German 1 Komm mit!, Chapter 4

Name _____ Klasse _____ Datum _____

KAPITEL 5 Klamotten kaufen

Alternative Quiz 5-1A

Erste Stufe

Maximum Score: 35

Grammar and Vocabulary

A. Write the German equivalents of the following names of colors. (7 points)

dark blue 1. _____
yellow   2. _____
black   3. _____
brown   4. _____
red   5. _____
green   6. _____
white   7. _____

SCORE ____

B. You are browsing in a clothing store and overhear parts of a conversation between a mother and her son. Choose a word from the three choices given in parentheses that agrees with the article given. (7 points)

SON   Ich möchte eine 8. _____. (Hose, Pulli, Gürtel)

MOTHER Dazu brauchst du ein 9. _____ (Hemd, Hose, Gürtel) oder einen

       10. _____. (Pulli, Jeans, Bluse)

SON   Der 11. _____, (Rock, Jacke, Pulli) ist teuer, aber das

       12. _____ (Hemd, Pulli, Hose) ist preiswert.

MOTHER Gut, dann kaufen wir das 13. _____ (Hemd, Jacke, T-Shirt) in

       Weiß und die 14. _____ (Gürtel, Hose, Stiefel) für 35 Euro.

SCORE ____

German 1 Komm mit!, Chapter 5 Student Make-Up Assignments **101**

Name _____ Klasse _____ Datum _____

Alternative Quiz 5-1A

C. Complete the following statements by filling in each blank with the correct form of the definite article. (10 points)

15. _____ Pulli kostet nur 30 Euro, aber 16. _____ Rock kostet 40 Euro.

17. _____ Kleid ist schick, aber 18. _____ Stiefel sehen blöd aus.

Heidi möchte 19. _____ Jogging-Anzug.

20. _____ Hose ist billig, und auch 21. _____ Bluse ist preiswert.

Du, 22. _____ Turnschuhe sind toll! Ich glaube, ich kaufe 23. _____ Turnschuhe.

Albert, findest du 24. _____ Gürtel nicht auch toll?

SCORE ☐

D. Complete the following fashion advice in a teen magazine by filling in each blank with the correct form of the indefinite article. Leave the space blank if no article is needed. (11 points)

Starke und preiswerte Klamotten für die Fete im Winter? Du brauchst

25. _____ Pulli in Weiß, 26. _____ Hose in Schwarz,

27. _____ Stiefel und 28. _____ Gürtel.

29. _____ Stirnband passt auch prima zu den Klamotten.

Für die Fete im Sommer brauchst du 30. _____ Hemd in Gelb,

31. _____ Turnschuhe und 32. _____ Hose in Grün.

33. _____ Gürtel passt gut dazu. 34. _____ Hemd in Gelb

ist nicht teuer. Auch 35. _____ Turnschuhe sind nicht teuer.

SCORE ☐

TOTAL SCORE ☐

102 Student Make-Up Assignments

German 1 Komm mit!, Chapter 5

KAPITEL 5 — Klamotten kaufen

Name _____ Klasse _____ Datum _____

Alternative Quiz 5-2A

Zweite Stufe

Maximum Score: 35

Grammar and Vocabulary

A. Your friend Heike needs a new dress and you accompany her to the *Modehaus Schick* and give your opinion on different dresses she tries on. Give the German equivalent of the response in parentheses. (15 points)

Gefällt dir das Kleid in Hellblau?

1. _____ (It does not fit.)

Ich finde das lange Kleid sehr fesch. Und du?

2. _____ (I'm not sure.)

Wie findest du das rote Kleid?

3. _____ (It is a little tight.)

Das grüne Kleid ist sehr preiswert. Findest du nicht?

4. _____ (No, it is expensive!)

Es passt auch prima.

5. _____ (I think it's really awesome!)

SCORE _____

B. Complete each of the following statements, using the German equivalents of the English cues given. (5 points)

Die Jacke ist 6. _____ . (too small)

Das Hemd ist 7. _____ . (too tight)

Die Stiefel sind 8. _____ . (too big)

Der Pulli ist 9. _____ . (too short)

Die Bluse ist 10. _____ . (too long)

SCORE _____

German 1 Komm mit!, Chapter 5　　Student Make-Up Assignments　**103**

Name _____ Klasse _____ Datum _____

Alternative Quiz 5-2A

C. Complete the following conversation, filling in each blank with an appropriate word from the word box. (10 points)

fesch	gefällt		passen		prima	zu eng	
	weiß	überhaupt		du		deine	Blau

MAX Du, Uwe, ich finde 11. _____ Stiefel echt toll. Sie

12. _____ gut zu deiner Hose. Dein Hemd in

13. _____ ist auch sehr 14. _____ . Es

15. _____ mir.

UWE Ich 16. _____ nicht. Findest 17. _____ es nicht

18. _____ ?

MAX Nein, 19. _____ nicht. Es passt 20. _____ .

SCORE ☐

D. Complete each of the following conversations, filling in the blanks with subject and direct object pronouns. (5 points)

A: Sag, Marika, gefällt dir der Rock?

B: Ja, 21. _____ gefällt mir. Ich finde 22. _____ sehr fesch.

A: Du, Holger, wie findest du die Stiefel?

B: Ich finde 23. _____ lässig.

A: Du, Hans, wie findest du den Pulli?

B: Ich finde 24. _____ toll, aber 25. _____ ist ein bisschen eng.

SCORE ☐

TOTAL SCORE ☐

Name _____ Klasse _____ Datum _____

KAPITEL 5 — Klamotten kaufen

Alternative Quiz 5-3A
Maximum Score: 30

Dritte Stufe

Grammar and Vocabulary

A. Write sentences, using all the cues given. (6 points)

Seine Turnschuhe / aussehen / lässig

1. _____

Ute / anziehen / ihren Jogging-Anzug

2. _____

Du / anprobieren / die blaue Jacke

3. _____

SCORE ☐

B. Complete the following conversations by filling in the blanks with appropriate forms of the verbs **nehmen** and **aussehen**. (12 points)

FRIEDA Die Jacke 4. _____ echt stark _____ .

EMMA Sie ist teuer, 5. _____ du sie?

FRIEDA Ja, ich 6. _____ sie.

HEIKO Glaubst du der Walter 7. _____ den Jogging-Anzug?

MARKUS Er 8. _____ ihn bestimmt. Er

9. _____ bequem _____ .

WALTER Ja, stimmt!

SCORE ☐

German 1 Komm mit!, Chapter 5 — Student Make-Up Assignments 105

Name _____ Klasse _____ Datum _____

Alternative Quiz 5-3A

C. Complete the following conversation, filling in each blank with an appropriate word from the word box. (6 points)

> Klamotten   brauche   weiß
>   du   Bluse   Modehaus Bügelfrei

ERIKA   Was ziehst 10. _____ zur Fete an?

SUSI   Ich 11. _____ nicht, meine 12. _____ sehen nicht fesch aus. Ich 13. _____ Jeans und eine neue 14. _____. Gehen wir zum 15. _____ und probieren Klamotten an?

ERIKA   Toll!

SCORE ____

D. At a party you overhear a conversation between Monika, Ulrike, and Antje about Inge. Read the dialogue below, and then answer the questions that follow.

MONIKA Inge sieht toll aus in dem blauen Kleid. Findet ihr nicht?
ANTJE   Ich weiß nicht. Das Kleid ist schick, aber ein bisschen kurz.
ULRIKE Mir gefällt dieses Kleid. Es sieht sehr teuer aus.
MONIKA Stimmt! Dieses blaue Kleid sieht wirklich lässig aus.
ULRIKE Es kostet bestimmt 100 Euro.
MONIKA Ich glaube, es kostet mehr.
ULRIKE Morgen kaufe ich dieses Kleid in Rot.

For each statement write the name of the person to whom it applies. (6 points)

16. _____ She finds Inge's dress too short.
17. _____ She is going to buy the same dress but in red.
18. _____ She thinks the dress costs 100 Euro.
19. _____ She finds the dress stylish.
20. _____ She finds the dress casual.
21. _____ She thinks that the dress costs more than 100 Euro.

SCORE ____

TOTAL SCORE ____

Name _____ Klasse _____ Datum _____

KAPITEL 6 — Pläne machen

Erste Stufe

Alternative Quiz 6-1A

Maximum Score: 30

Grammar and Vocabulary

A. Write the German equivalent of each of these English phrases. (5 points)

How are you?	1. _____
Miserable.	2. _____
Okay.	3. _____
Bad.	4. _____
Very well!	5. _____

SCORE ☐

B. Match each phrase on the right with the correct time on the left. (10 points)

6. _____ 6.15
7. _____ 10.30
8. _____ 1.20
9. _____ 8.45
10. _____ 9.05
11. _____ 7.55
12. _____ 6.10
13. _____ 12.30
14. _____ 2.15
15. _____ 3.45

a. halb elf
b. zwanzig nach eins
c. zehn nach sechs
d. Viertel vor vier
e. halb eins
f. fünf vor acht
g. Viertel nach sechs
h. fünf nach neun
i. Viertel nach zwei
j. Viertel vor neun

SCORE ☐

German 1 Komm mit!, Chapter 6   Student Make-Up Assignments   **107**

Copyright © by Holt, Rinehart and Winston. All rights reserved.

Name _____ Klasse _____ Datum _____

Alternative Quiz 6-1A

C. Write out the appropriate time using informal time expressions. (10 points)

10.15   **16.** _____

9.30   **17.** _____

11.45   **18.** _____

2.30   **19.** _____

1.45   **20.** _____

D. Read Erika's schedule for Wednesday and then answer the questions below the schedule. (5 points)

MITTWOCH	
8.00	Englisch
9.45	Erdkunde
10.30	Pause
11.15	Geschichte
1.30	Physik

Write out the appropriate time using informal time expressions.

Wann hat Erika Erdkunde?   **21.** _____

Wann hat Erika Pause?   **22.** _____

Wann hat Erika Physik?   **23.** _____

Wann hat Erika Geschichte?   **24.** _____

Wann hat Erika Englisch?   **25.** _____

SCORE ☐

TOTAL SCORE ☐

KAPITEL 6

Student Make-Up Assignments   German 1 Komm mit!, Chapter 6

KAPITEL 6 — Pläne machen

Name _____ Klasse _____ Datum _____

Zweite Stufe

Alternative Quiz 6-2A
Maximum Score: 35

Grammar and Vocabulary

A. Fill in the blanks with the appropriate place, using the cues given. (5 points)

Angelika geht   1. _____ (downtown).
Peter geht morgen   2. _____ (to a café).
Wir gehen heute   3. _____ (to the movies).
Uwe geht am Wochenende   4. _____ (to the pool).
Heike geht am Freitag   5. _____ (to a concert).

SCORE ____

B. Paul and Michael are talking about their weekend plans. Fill in the correct forms of the verb **wollen**. (12 points)

PAUL   Was 6. _____ du am Samstag machen?

MICHAEL Ich 7. _____ ins Kino gehen. 8. _____ du mitkommen?

PAUL   Nein, danke. Ich 9. _____ ins Schwimmbad gehen, und am Abend 10. _____ der Uwe und ich Karten spielen.

MICHAEL Wie du 11. _____ .

SCORE ____

German 1 Komm mit!, Chapter 6   Student Make-Up Assignments **109**

Name _____ Klasse _____ Datum _____

Alternative Quiz 6-2A

C. Describe your daily routine by filling in each blank with the appropriate word from the word box. (10 points)

meine Karten zuerst besuche nach Hause
Donnerstag hören Dann Hausaufgaben gehe

Ich gehe 12. _____ in die Schule. Am Montag, Dienstag, und

13. _____ habe ich um 8 Uhr Deutsch.

14. _____ habe ich Mathe und Englisch. Nach der Schule

15. _____ ich ins Schwimmbad. Dann gehe ich

16. _____ und mache 17. _____. Danach

18. _____ ich 19. _____ Freunde. Wir

20. _____ Musik oder spielen 21. _____.

SCORE ____

D. Give the German equivalents of the sentences below. Be sure to use the correct verb form. (8 points)

We want to play soccer.

22. _____

Markus and Udo want to eat ice cream.

23. _____

You want to go downtown?

24. _____

When does Heike want to do the homework?

25. _____

SCORE ____

TOTAL SCORE ____

110   Student Make-Up Assignments   German 1 Komm mit!, Chapter 6

Name _____ Klasse _____ Datum _____

KAPITEL 6 Pläne machen

Alternative Quiz 6-3A

Dritte Stufe

Maximum Score: 35

Grammar and Vocabulary

A. Write the German equivalents of the following English phrases. (10 points)

How does it taste?   1. _____.
The check please!   2. _____.
That comes to EUR 13,50. 3. _____.
Watch out!   4. _____.
Great!   5. _____.

SCORE _____

B. You and your friends Albert and Horst talk about ordering food in the Café *Mokka.* Fill in each blank with the correct form of the indefinite article. (10 points)

Ich bekomme 6. _____ Wurstbrot und 7. _____ Glas Apfelsaft.

Danach esse ich 8. _____ Eis und trinke 9. _____ Tasse Kaffee.

Albert, was bekommst du? Ich bekomme nur 10. _____ Nudelsuppe und

11. _____ Glas Tee mit Zitrone. Was bekommst du, Horst? Ich bekomme

12. _____ Pizza und 13. _____ Limonade. Danach bekomme ich

14. _____ Apfelkuchen und 15. _____ Mineralwasser.

SCORE _____

C. Match each answer on the left with the appropriate question on the right. (5 points)

16. _____ Er möchte eine Pizza.   a. Was willst du machen?
17. _____ Lecker!   b. Was machst du am Wochenende?
18. _____ Er kostet EUR 4,50.   c. Wie schmeckt das Käsebrot?
19. _____ Ich will baden gehen.   d. Was möchte Uwe?
20. _____ Ich gehe am Sonntag wandern.   e. Was kostet der Eisbecher?

SCORE _____

German 1 Komm mit!, Chapter 6   Student Make-Up Assignments   **111**

Name _____ Klasse _____ Datum _____

Alternative Quiz 6-3A

D. Fill in the correct forms of the missing verbs using the verbs from the word box. Use each word only once. (10 points)

| bekommen | wollen | stimmen | machen | gehen |
| brauchen | schmecken | zahlen | kaufen | essen |

MORITZ Max, was **21.** _____ du heute nach der Schule?

MAX Ich **22.** _____ nach Hause.

MORITZ **23.** _____ du zuerst ins *Café Mokka* gehen?

MAX Ja, gern! Ich **24.** _____ gern ein Eis.

MORITZ Ich auch!

(im *Café Mokka*)

MAX Ich **25.** _____ ein Eis.

MORITZ Ich bekomme zuerst ein Mineralwasser, und dann will ich auch einen Eisbecher.

MAX Wie **26.** _____ dein Eis?

MORITZ Sehr gut! Und dein Eis?

MAX Lecker.

MORITZ Hallo! Wir möchten **27.** _____ , bitte!

WAITER Das macht zusammen EUR 7,50.

MORITZ **28.** _____ schon! Gehen wir, Max?

MORITZ Ja. Ich will ein neues T-Shirt **29.** _____ , für die Fete am Samstag.

MAX Ich **30.** _____ auch ein neues T-Shirt und eine Shorts.

MORITZ Prima! Fahren wir in die Stadt.

SCORE ☐

TOTAL SCORE ☐

KAPITEL 7 — Zu Hause helfen

Erste Stufe

Alternative Quiz 7-1A
Maximum Score: 30

Grammar and Vocabulary

A. What types of housework do these students do? Fill in each blank with an appropriate word or expression from the word box. Be sure to give the correct form of the verbs. (15 points)

füttern	Klamotten	putzen	spülen	die Katze	Staub
saugen	gießen	decken	mähen		
mein Zimmer	sortieren	machen	die Blumen	helfen	

INGRID Ich helfe nicht viel zu Hause. Ich räume meine 1. _____ auf, und 2. _____ Staub.

BARBARA Ich helfe sehr viel zu Hause. Ich 3. _____ die Blumen, ich 4. _____ das Geschirr, ich sauge 5. _____ und ich 6. _____ den Tisch.

FRANZ Ich 7. _____ auch viel zu Hause. Ich räume 8. _____ auf, ich 9. _____ die Fenster, ich 10. _____ das Bett und füttere 11. _____ .

HANS Ich helfe auch viel zu Hause. Ich gieße 12. _____ , ich 13. _____ die Katze, ich 14. _____ den Müll und ich 15. _____ den Rasen.

SCORE _____

B. Complete each of these brief conversations by filling in the first two blanks with correct forms of **müssen,** and the third one with the appropriate infinitive. (6 points)

A: Was 16. _____ du am Montag machen?

B: Ich 17. _____ den Müll _____ .

Name _____ Klasse _____ Datum _____

Alternative Quiz 7-1A

A: Was 18. _____ wir am Samstag tun?

B: Wir 19. _____ den Rasen _____.

A: Was 20. _____ ich heute tun?

B: Du 21. _____ dein Zimmer _____.

SCORE ☐

C. What are these students doing? Write sentences in the present tense, using all the information given. (3 points)

Bruno / abräumen / den Tisch

22. _____

Marolda / aufräumen / das Zimmer

23. _____

Peter / anprobieren / das Hemd

24. _____

SCORE ☐

D. Write the German equivalents of the following English phrases. (6 points)

That won't work.   25. _____

Sorry, I can't.   26. _____

Why don't you come along? 27. _____

SCORE ☐

TOTAL SCORE ☐

114 Student Make-Up Assignments   German 1 Komm mit!, Chapter 7

Copyright © by Holt, Rinehart and Winston. All rights reserved.

Name _____ Klasse _____ Datum _____

7 Zu Hause helfen

Zweite Stufe

Alternative Quiz 7-2A

Maximum Score: 40

Grammar and Vocabulary

A. Write the German equivalents of the following expressions. (10 points)

about three times a month	1. _____
every day	2. _____
five times a week	3. _____
twice a month	4. _____
How often?	5. _____

SCORE ☐

B. Your parents tell you and your sister Susan what your chores are in the coming week. Complete each of the following sentences by filling in the first blank with the appropriate form of **können** and the second blank with the appropriate infinitive. (10 points)

Susan 6. _____ ihr Zimmer _____ .

Ihr 7. _____ die Fenster _____ .

Susan 8. _____ den Rasen _____ .

Ihr 9. _____ die Blumen _____ .

Du 10. _____ die Katze _____ .

SCORE ☐

German 1 Komm mit!, Chapter 7 Student Make-Up Assignments **115**

Name _____ Klasse _____ Datum _____

Alternative Quiz 7-2A

C. Answer the following questions in complete sentences, using the German equivalents of the English cues given. (10 points)

Für wen sind die Blumen?

11. _____ (for her)

Für wen ist der Apfelkuchen?

12. _____ (for us)

Für wen ist die neue Hose?

13. _____ (for you, sg., informal)

Für wen ist die Pizza?

14. _____ (for me)

Für wen ist der Tisch?

15. _____ (for you, pl.)

SCORE ____

D. Your grandmother is going on vacation and you ask her what you and your brother Heinz can do in order to take care of her house. Fill in the blanks with appropriate forms of **können,** appropriate infinitives, and the appropriate pronouns. (10 points)

YOU Oma, was 16. _____ wir für 17. _____ tun?

OMA Ihr 18. _____ für 19. _____ den Rasen

20. _____ . Heinz, du 21. _____ meine Katze

22. _____ .

HEINZ Gut, Oma. Ich 23. _____ auch den Müll

24. _____ und die Fenster 25. _____ .

OMA Prima! Ich muss dann öfter in Urlaub fahren.

SCORE ____

TOTAL SCORE ____

Name _____ Klasse _____ Datum _____

KAPITEL 7 Zu Hause helfen

Dritte Stufe

Alternative Quiz 7-3A

Maximum Score: 30

Grammar and Vocabulary

A. Write the German equivalent next to each English weather expression. (10 points)

It's hot and dry in August.

1. _____

How is the weather in March?

2. _____

It's cold and wet in January.

3. _____

What's the temperature?

4. _____

It's raining today.

5. _____

SCORE ☐

B. Match each weather report on the left with an appropriate activity on the right. (5 points)

6. _____ Es regnet.   a. ins Schwimmbad gehen
7. _____ Es gibt ein Gewitter.   b. Ski laufen
8. _____ Es ist kühl und sonnig.   c. Schach spielen
9. _____ Es schneit.   d. nicht Golf spielen
10. _____ Es ist heiß und trocken. e. wandern

SCORE ☐

German 1 Komm mit!, Chapter 7   Student Make-Up Assignments   **117**

Name _____ Klasse _____ Datum _____

Alternative Quiz 7-3A

C. Match each question on the left with the appropriate answer on the right. (5 points)

11. _____ Wie viel Grad haben wir heute?   a. Ja, oft.
12. _____ Ist es im Juli heiß in Arizona?   b. Ungefähr 15 Grad.
13. _____ Habt ihr im August oft Gewitter?   c. Morgen schneit es bestimmt.
14. _____ Schneit es morgen?   d. Kalt und nass.
15. _____ Wie ist das Wetter im Dezember?   e. Ja, sehr heiß.

SCORE [ ]

D. Maria, who lives in Munich, plans to visit her friend Pamela in Texas. She calls Pamela to find out what the weather is like in Texas. Fill in the blanks in their conversation with appropriate words or expressions from the word box. (10 points)

| das Wetter | regnet | heute | trocken | Schwimmbad |
| kühl | sehr heiß | 20 Grad | baden | der Wetterbericht |

MARIA Hallo Pamela! Wie geht's? Wie ist 16. _____ in Texas? Was sagt 17. _____ ?

PAMELA Hallo! Das Wetter ist toll! Es ist heute 18. _____ . Wir haben 35 Grad im Schatten. Es 19. _____ nicht, und es ist sehr trocken.

MARIA Prima! Hier in München regnet es 20. _____ , und es ist ein bisschen 21. _____ . Wir haben ungefähr 22. _____ . Morgen ist es warm und 23. _____ . Du gehst bestimmt in Texas oft 24. _____ ?

PAMELA Ja, ich gehe oft ins 25. _____ .

MARIA Ich freue mich schon sehr auf meinen Besuch. Bis dann!

PAMELA Tschüs.

SCORE [ ]
TOTAL SCORE [ ]

118 Student Make-Up Assignments   German 1 Komm mit!, Chapter 7

KAPITEL 8

Name _____ Klasse _____ Datum _____

Einkaufen gehen

Alternative Quiz 8-1A

Erste Stufe

Maximum Score: 30

Grammar and Vocabulary

A. Your grandmother asks you to do her shopping. Complete the following conversation by filling in the blanks with the appropriate words from the word box. Make sure to use the correct form of the verbs. (10 points)

Bäcker	Brot	ein Hähnchen	Torte	sollen	
EUR 20	Gemüseladen	dich	gehen	kaufen

DU Du, Oma, 1. _____ ich für 2. _____ einkaufen gehen?

OMA Ach, kauf 3. _____ im Supermarkt.

DU Soll ich es nicht beim 4. _____ kaufen? Dort ist es frisch.

OMA Prima! Kauf dir dort auch ein Stück 5. _____ .

DU Gut, Oma. Sonst noch etwas?

OMA Ja, 6. _____ zum Metzger und kauf

7. _____ . Dann geh zum 8. _____

und 9. _____ Tomaten und Kartoffeln! Hier, nimm

10. _____ mit!

SCORE _____

B. Complete the following statements by filling in each blank with the correct form of the definite article. (10 points)

Im Supermarkt kaufe ich 11. _____ Käse, 12. _____ Kaffee,

13. _____ Butter, und 14. _____ Eier.

Beim Bäcker kaufe ich 15. _____ Brot und 16. _____ Brezeln.

Im Obstladen kaufe ich 17. _____ Trauben und 18. _____ Äpfel.

Beim Metzger kaufe ich 19. _____ Wurst und 20. _____ Hackfleisch.

SCORE _____

German 1 Komm mit!, Chapter 8   Student Make-Up Assignments

Name _____ Klasse _____ Datum _____

Alternative Quiz 8-1A

C. Match each question on the left with the appropriate answer on the right. (5 points)

21. _____ Willst du einkaufen gehen?   a. Ja, das kannst du machen.
22. _____ Kann ich für dich den Rasen mähen?   b. Im Supermarkt
23. _____ Wo kaufst du die Milch?   c. Ich habe heute keine Zeit.
24. _____ Was soll die Ulrike beim Metzger kaufen?   d. Aufschnitt und Fleisch
25. _____ Was soll ich für dich tun?   e. Geh bitte zum Bäcker!

SCORE _____

D. Write the German equivalent next to each English item. (5 points)

at the café

26. _____

at the produce store

27. _____

at the baker's

28. _____

at the butcher's

29. _____

at the supermarket

30. _____

SCORE _____

TOTAL SCORE _____

Name _____ Klasse _____ Datum _____

KAPITEL 8 Einkaufen gehen

Zweite Stufe

Alternative Quiz 8-2A

Maximum Score: 35

Grammar and Vocabulary

A. Complete the following conversation at the bakery by filling in the blanks with appropriate words or phrases. (5 points)

VERKÄUFER Guten Morgen! Kann ich Ihnen 1. _____ ?

FRAU BAUER Ja, bitte. Ich bekomme zehn Semmeln und ein Brot.

VERKÄUFER Hier, bitte. 2. _____ Sie noch einen Wunsch?

FRAU BAUER Ich brauche 3. _____ fünf Brezeln.

VERKÄUFER Sonst noch 4. _____ ?

FRAU BAUER Nein, danke. Das ist 5. _____ .

VERKÄUFER Auf Wiedersehen!

FRAU BAUER Wiedersehen!

SCORE ☐

B. Write in German what you still need, using the English cues given. (5 points)

A: Was braucht ihr noch?
B: Wir brauchen noch

6. _____ (cheese and butter)

7. _____ (one kilo of potatoes)

8. _____ (250 grams of cold cuts)

9. _____ (one liter of milk)

10. _____ (two pounds of grapes)

SCORE ☐

German 1 Komm mit!, Chapter 8   Student Make-Up Assignments **121**

Name _____ Klasse _____ Datum _____

Alternative Quiz 8-2A

C. Write the German equivalent of each English sentence. (15 points)

Would you like anything else?

11. _____

I also need a pound of ground meat.

12. _____

How many rolls do you buy at the baker's?

13. _____

I need a little more flour.

14. _____

That's all. Thank you.

15. _____

SCORE [ ]

D. Complete the following conversation by filling in the first blank with the correct form of the definite article, and the second with the correct form of the pronoun. (10 points)

A: Wie viel wiegt 16. _____ Wurst?

B: 17. _____ wiegt 250 Gramm.

A: Wie viel wiegt 18. _____ Aufschnitt?

B: 19. _____ wiegt 500 Gramm.

A: Wie viel wiegen 20. _____ Trauben?

B: 21. _____ wiegen 2 Kilo.

A: Wie viel wiegt 22. _____ Fisch?

B: 23. _____ wiegt 4 Pfund.

A: Wie viel wiegen 24. _____ Kartoffeln?

B: 25. _____ wiegen 5 Kilo.

SCORE [ ]

TOTAL SCORE [ ]

Name _____ Klasse _____ Datum _____

KAPITEL 8 Einkaufen gehen

Alternative Quiz 8-3A

Dritte Stufe

Maximum Score: 35

Grammar and Vocabulary

A. Match each question on the left with the appropriate answer on the right. (5 points)

1. _____ Wo wart ihr gestern?
2. _____ Was soll ich kaufen?
3. _____ Wie viel Hackfleisch bekommen Sie?
4. _____ Haben Sie noch einen Wunsch?
5. _____ Was kann ich für dich tun?

a. Deck den Tisch!
b. Nein, danke.
c. Wir waren im Kino.
d. Mehl und Zucker
e. 500 Gramm, bitte!

SCORE _____

B. Write the German equivalent of each English sentence. (15 points)

We were at the movies yesterday evening.

6. _____

He was at the butcher's this afternoon.

7. _____

I was at home the day before yesterday.

8. _____

Heike has to go shopping tomorrow, because she needs milk.

9. _____

They were in Berlin last weekend.

10. _____

SCORE _____

German 1 Komm mit!, Chapter 8   Student Make-Up Assignments   **123**

Name _____ Klasse _____ Datum _____

Alternative Quiz 8-3A

C. A detective with the police department in Stuttgart asks a suspect in a robbery about his whereabouts at the time of the crime. Complete the following interview by filling in the blanks with the correct past tense form of **sein** and appropriate words from the word box. (10 points)

> halb   Film   Gladiator
> wie viel   im Kino   gestern Abend

DETECTIVE   Wo 11. _____ Sie 12. _____ ?

SUSPECT   Ich 13. _____ zuerst 14. _____ und dann im *Café Expresso.*

DETECTIVE   Welchen 15. _____ haben Sie gesehen?

SUSPECT   Ich habe 16. _____ gesehen.

DETECTIVE   Um 17. _____ Uhr?

SUSPECT   Um 18. _____ acht.

DETECTIVE   Sie 19. _____ nicht in der Bundesbank?

SUSPECT   Nein! Mein Freund Uwe und ich 20. _____ im Kino.

DETECTIVE   Vielen Dank für Ihre Hilfe. Auf Wiedersehen!

SCORE [ ]

D. Connect the following sentences with the conjunction **weil.** (5 points)

Heidi war in der *Boutique Schick.* Die Blusen sind dort preiswert.

21. _____

Peter geht heute ins Schwimmbad. Es ist sehr heiß.

22. _____

Ich war gestern nicht in der Schule. Ich war krank.

23. _____

Sie geht nicht ins Kino. Sie hat kein Geld.

24. _____

Antje hat die Semmeln beim Bäcker gekauft. Sie sind dort frisch.

25. _____

SCORE [ ]   TOTAL SCORE [ ]

Name _____ Klasse _____ Datum _____

KAPITEL 9 Amerikaner in München

Erste Stufe

Alternative Quiz 9-1A

Maximum Score: 30

Grammar and Vocabulary

A. Give the English equivalent of each German noun phrase. (5 points)

1. _____ der Garten
2. _____ das Rathaus
3. _____ der Marktplatz
4. _____ die Kirche
5. _____ das Museum

SCORE _____

B. Complete each of the following questions or answers by filling in the blanks with the correct form of the verb **wissen**. (10 points)

A: Maria und Linda, 6. _____ ihr, wo das Rathaus ist?

B: Ja, wir 7. _____ es.

A: Günther, 8. _____ du, wo die U-Bahnstation ist?

B: Nein, das 9. _____ ich nicht.

A: 10. _____ die Hilde und die Heike, wo das Museum ist?

B: Ja, sie 11. _____ es.

A: 12. _____ die Erika, wo der Englische Garten ist?

B: Nein, sie 13. _____ es nicht.

A: Entschuldigung, 14. _____ Sie, wo der Bahnhof ist?

B: Ja, das 15. _____ ich.

SCORE _____

German 1 Komm mit!, Chapter 9   Student Make-Up Assignments   **125**

Name _____ Klasse _____ Datum _____

Alternative Quiz 9-1A

C. Using the cues given, ask the following people if they know where different locations are in the city. (15 points)

Anneliese, the church

16. _____

Markus und Erika, the post office

17. _____

Frau Hinterhofer, the hotel

18. _____

Max, the theater

19. _____

Herr Hinterhuber, the bank

20. _____

SCORE ☐

TOTAL SCORE ☐

Name _____ Klasse _____ Datum _____

KAPITEL 9 Amerikaner in München

Alternative Quiz 9-2A

Zweite Stufe

Maximum Score: 35

Grammar and Vocabulary

A. Several people have asked you for directions to various places in the city. Complete the sentences by filling in the correct command form of the verb **gehen** or **fahren**. (16 points)

Das Karlstor ist nicht weit von hier, in der Fußgängerzone. 1. _____ Sie die erste Straße nach rechts, dann die zweite Straße nach links.

Der Englische Garten ist ungefähr drei Kilometer von hier, Klaus. 2. _____ mit dem Rad! 3. _____ nach rechts hier in die Ludwigstraße und nach ungefähr einem Kilometern in die Schönfeldstraße!

Der Supermarkt ist weit von hier. 4. _____ Sie mit dem Bus dorthin!

Die Bank ist nur fünf Minuten (mit dem Auto) von hier. 5. _____ Sie bis zur Ampel, und dann 6. _____ Sie nach links in die Bäckerstraße! Dort ist sie auf der rechten Seite.

Aber Max und Inge, das Haus der Kunst ist ganz in der Nähe! 7. _____ zu Fuß geradeaus bis zur nächsten Ecke, dann 8. _____ nach links in die Königinstraße, und da ist es direkt vor euch!

SCORE ____

German 1 Komm mit!, Chapter 9   Student Make-Up Assignments **127**

Copyright © by Holt, Rinehart and Winston. All rights reserved.

Name _____ Klasse _____ Datum _____

Alternative Quiz 9-2A

B. Fill in the blanks with the correct command form and the correct form of **zu**. (6 points)

   Tell Ms. White, your German teacher, to walk straight ahead to the traffic light.

   9. _____ geradeaus bis 10. _____ Ampel!

   Tell your friend Ingrid to take the bus to school.

   11. _____ mit dem Bus 12. _____ Schule!

   Tell Michael and Gisela to go to the right (driving) until they get to the market square.

   13. _____ nach links bis 14. _____ Marktplatz!

SCORE _____

C. You are giving directions to various people. Complete the sentences by filling in the blanks with the correct command form of the verb **gehen** and the correct form of **zu** plus the definite article. (13 points)

(You are talking to friends.)

Ihr wollt 15. _____ Supermarkt? 16. _____ nur um die Ecke!

Wenn ihr 17. _____ Rathaus wollt, 18. _____ zuerst nach links,

und 19. _____ dann immer geradeaus bis zur Hirtengasse!

Ihr möchtet 20. _____ Bank gehen? Dann 21. _____ die dritte

Straße nach links und da ist die Sparkasse.

(You are talking to an elderly gentleman.)

22. _____ Sie bis 23. _____ Karolinenplatz, und

24. _____ Sie dann nach links in die Briennerstraße!

(You are talking to a schoolchild.)

25. _____ bis 26. _____ Post, dann geradeaus bis

27. _____ Michaelistraße.

SCORE _____

TOTAL SCORE _____

128   Student Make-Up Assignments   German 1 Komm mit!, Chapter 9

KAPITEL 9 Amerikaner in München

Dritte Stufe

Alternative Quiz 9-3A

Maximum Score: 35

Grammar and Vocabulary

A. The waiter at an **Imbissstube** is asking you if you want another of what you have been eating or drinking. Complete his questions by filling in the correct form of **noch ein** and the vocabulary word required. (12 points)

Möchten Sie 1. _____ 2. _____ ? (sausage)

Möchten Sie 3. _____ 4. _____ ? (apple juice)

Möchten Sie 5. _____ 6. _____ ? (mineral water)

Möchten Sie 7. _____ 8. _____ ? (ice cream)

Möchten Sie 9. _____ 10. _____ ? (roll)

Möchten Sie 11. _____ 12. _____ ? (gyros)

SCORE ____

B. Complete the following conversations by filling in **es gibt** or **gibt es**. (7 points)

HEIDI 13. _____ heute Pizza?

ERWIN Nein, 14. _____ heute Leberkäs.

HEIDI Wo 15. _____ hier ein Kino?

ERWIN Ein Kino 16. _____ hier nicht.

HEIDI 17. _____ Käsekuchen im *Café Hubertus*?

ERWIN Aber ja! 18. _____ auch Eis. 19. _____ dort sogar Maracujaeis!

SCORE ____

German 1 Komm mit!, Chapter 9 Student Make-Up Assignments

Name _____ Klasse _____ Datum _____

Alternative Quiz 9-3A

C. Complete the answers by filling in the correct form of **kein.** (8 points)

Gibt es noch Leberkäs? Nein, es gibt 20. _____ Leberkäs mehr.

Gibt es noch Semmeln? Nein, es gibt 21. _____ Semmeln mehr.

Gibt es noch Pizza? Nein, es gibt 22. _____ Pizza mehr.

Gibt es noch Tomaten? Nein, es gibt 23. _____ Tomaten mehr.

SCORE ☐

D. Rewrite the following questions as affirmative statements. Use a **dass**-clause following the introductory phrase, **Du weißt,** …. (8 points)

Gibt es noch Kartoffeln?

Du weißt, dass 24. _____

War der Holger im Supermarkt?

Du weißt, dass 25. _____

Gibt es heute Eis?

Du weißt, dass 26. _____

Geht die Elfriede zum Gemüseladen?

Du weißt, dass 27. _____

SCORE ☐

TOTAL SCORE ☐

Kino und Konzerte

Erste Stufe

Alternative Quiz 10-1A

Maximum Score: 40

Grammar and Vocabulary

A. Complete the following questions by filling in the blanks with the correct form of the verb **wissen** or the verb **kennen**. (10 points)

1. _____ ihr den neuen Mathelehrer?
2. _____ du, dass ich gern Fußball spiele?
3. _____ Sie, Herr Mager, wann das National Museum offen ist?
4. _____ der Friedrich, dass er zum Bahnhof fahren muss?
5. _____ deine Eltern deine Freundin Erika?
6. _____ du *Die Zauberflöte* von Mozart?

Ja, ich 7. _____ die Schauspielerin.

Du 8. _____ meine Großeltern, nicht wahr?

Du 9. _____ , dass meine Mutter nicht gern kocht.

10. _____ ihr, wo ich den neuen Film sehen kann?

SCORE [ ]

B. Using the English cues given, ask three friends what they like. (9 points)

Marolda, do you like classical music?

11. _____

Albert, what kind of movies do you like?

12. _____

Heino, do you like war movies?

13. _____

SCORE [ ]

Name _____ Klasse _____ Datum _____

Alternative Quiz 10-1A

C. Complete the following questions and answers by filling in the blanks with the correct form of the verb **mögen** and the correct vocabulary word for the English in parentheses. (15 points)

DU   Frau Meindl, was 14. _____ Sie lieber?

15. _____ (comedies) oder 16. _____ ? (romances)

DU   Was für Filme 17. _____ du, Heike?

HEIKE   Ich 18. _____ 19. _____ (horror movies) und 20. _____ . (detective movies)

DU   Suzanne, was für Filme 21. _____ ihr am liebsten?

SUZANNE   Wir 22. _____ 23. _____ (adventure films) gern, aber am liebsten 24. _____ wir 25. _____ (science fiction movies).

DU   26. _____ Sie lieber 27. _____ (western movies) oder 28. _____ ? (horror movies)

SCORE ☐

D. Complete the following questions in German, according to whether the thing or person(s) mentioned is a film, a song, an actor or actress, a singer, or a group. (6 points)

Kennst du 29. _____ Gladiator?

Kennst du 30. _____ Tom Cruise?

Kennst du 31. _____ Julia Roberts?

Kennst du 32. _____ Britney Spears?

Kennst du 33. _____ U2?

Kennst du 34. _____ America the Beautiful?

SCORE ☐

TOTAL SCORE ☐

132   Student Make-Up Assignments   German 1 Komm mit!, Chapter 10

Name _____ Klasse _____ Datum _____

KAPITEL 10 Kino und Konzerte

Alternative Quiz 10-2A

zweite Stufe

Maximum Score: 30

Grammar and Vocabulary

A. What kinds of films do you and your friends like to see? Fill in the blanks with the correct form of the verb **sehen**. (14 points)

Dein Bruder 1. _____ nur Krimis, nicht wahr?

Warum 2. _____ deine Kusine nur Liebesfilme?

Was für Filme 3. _____ ihr gern, Rudi und Karl?

Ich 4. _____ besonders gern Actionfilme.

Was für Filme 5. _____ deine Eltern gern, Andrea?

Wir alle 6. _____ Komödien sehr gern.

Was für Filme 7. _____ du gern?

SCORE _____

B. What do you like? What do you prefer? What do you like most of all? Complete the following sentences by filling in the blanks with the appropriate words to express likes, preferences, and favorites. (6 points)

Ich mag 8. _____ Sciencefictionfilme. (like)

Ich mag Abenteuerfilme 9. _____ . (prefer)

Aber 10. _____ mag ich Krimis! (favorite)

SCORE _____

German 1 Komm mit!, Chapter 10   Student Make-Up Assignments   **133**

Name _____ Klasse _____ Datum _____

Alternative Quiz 10-2A

C. Write the German equivalents in the blanks to the left of the English words. (10 points)

_____	11. bad	spannend
_____	12. imaginative	dumm
_____	13. thrilling	sensationell
_____	14. sensational	schlecht
_____	15. stupid	traurig
_____	16. corny	grausam
_____	17. sad	brutal
_____	18. cruel	schmalzig
_____	19. violent	phantasievoll
_____	20. funny	lustig

SCORE _____

TOTAL SCORE _____

KAPITEL 10

134 Student Make-Up Assignments   German 1 Komm mit!, Chapter 10

Name _____ Klasse _____ Datum _____

KAPITEL 10 Kino und Konzerte

Alternative Quiz 10-3A

Dritte Stufe

Maximum Score: 30

Grammar and Vocabulary

A. What kinds of books are you and your friends reading? Complete the following sentences by filling in the blanks with the correct form of the verb **lesen**. (7 points)

Monika 1. _____ ein Hobbybuch.

Meine Mutter 2. _____ die Zeitung.

Was 3. _____ ihr, Holger und Katrin?

Meine Schwester 4. _____ einen Liebesroman.

Frau Knapp, was 5. _____ Sie?

Steffi, was 6. _____ du?

Die Großeltern 7. _____ Romane.

SCORE _____

B. Your friends have asked what you and your family did during summer vacation. Complete the following answers by filling in the blanks with the correct German past tense form of the verb in parentheses. (5 points)

Im August 8. _____ (to be) wir in Italien. Wir haben viel gefaulenzt, aber wir haben auch viel 9. _____ (to do).

In Italien habe ich einen tollen Film 10. _____ (to see). Später habe ich mit meinen Freunden über den Film 11. _____ (to speak). Ich habe auch viele Bücher 12. _____ (to read).

SCORE _____

German 1 Komm mit!, Chapter 10 Student Make-Up Assignments **135**

Name _____ Klasse _____ Datum _____

Alternative Quiz 10-3A

C. Give the German equivalents of the following questions and statements, using a **wo**-compound to introduce the questions. (18 points)

What are you talking about? (informal singular)

13. _____

What are you talking about? (informal plural)

14. _____

I am talking about politics.

15. _____

Uwe is talking about the adventure movie.

16. _____

My parents are talking about the weather.

17. _____

We are talking about fashion.

18. _____

They are talking about the environment.

19. _____

About whom are you (informal plural) talking?

20. _____

Elke is talking about the horror novel.

21. _____

SCORE ☐

TOTAL SCORE ☐

Name _____ Klasse _____ Datum _____

KAPITEL 11 Der Geburtstag

Erste Stufe

Alternative Quiz 11-1A

Maximum Score: 30

Grammar and Vocabulary

A. Complete the following conversations by filling in the blanks with the correct form of the verb **anrufen**. (8 points)

A: Meine Eltern wollen wissen, wen ich 1. _____ !

A: 2. _____ du die Oma 3. _____ ?

B: Ja, ich 4. _____ sie 5. _____ .

A: Frau Huber, 6. _____ Sie Frau Hermann 7. _____ ?

B: Nein, heute nicht. Ich werde sie erst morgen 8. _____ .

SCORE _____

B. Using the words in the box below, unscramble the instructions on telephone use. Each word or phrase is used only once. (10 points)

> Telefonieren   den Apparat   in die Telefonzelle gehen   sprechen
> den Hörer auflegen   Kann   besetzt
> den Hörer abheben   die Münzen einstecken   die Telefonnummer wählen

9. _____ ist leicht! Zuerst müssen Sie

10. _____ . Dann müssen Sie

11. _____ . Danach müssen Sie

12. _____ . Dann müssen Sie

13. _____ .

Wenn jemand an 14. _____ kommt, dann müssen Sie sagen:

15. _____ ich bitte Herrn oder Frau Soundso

16. _____ ?

Wenn 17. _____ ist, müssen Sie

18. _____ .

SCORE _____

German 1 Komm mit!, Chapter 11   Student Make-Up Assignments

Name _____ Klasse _____ Datum _____

Alternative Quiz 11-1A

C. When talking on the phone in German, how would you say the following? (12 points)

Goodbye.

19. _____

Just a minute, please.

20. _____

The Blum residence.

21. _____

This is Ms. Hinterhuber.

22. _____

SCORE ☐

TOTAL SCORE ☐

Der Geburtstag

KAPITEL 11

Alternative Quiz 11-2A
Maximum Score: 40

Zweite Stufe

Grammar and Vocabulary

A. When do the following people have birthdays? Complete the following sentences by filling in the blanks with the correct form of the ordinal numbers. (20 points)

Konnie hat am 1. _____ Geburtstag. (October 12)

Erwin hat am 2. _____ Geburtstag. (March 7)

Peter und Klara haben am 3. _____ Geburtstag. (May 8)

Sie hat am 4. _____ Geburtstag. (February 25)

Frau Erikson hat am 5. _____ Geburtstag. (July 17)

Michael hat am 6. _____ Geburtstag. (August 8)

Am 7. _____ hat Uwe Geburtstag. (June 28)

Am 8. _____ hat Ilona Geburtstag. (April 11)

Andreas hat am 9. _____ Geburtstag. (December 7)

Sara hat am 10. _____ Geburtstag. (March 15)

SCORE _____

B. Give the German equivalents for the following English sentences. (20 points)

Happy Birthday!

11. _____

Happy Mother's Day!

12. _____

Happy Father's Day!

13. _____

Happy Hanukkah!

14. _____

German 1 Komm mit!, Chapter 11   Student Make-Up Assignments   **139**

Alternative Quiz 11-2A

When is her birthday?

15. _____

Merry Christmas!

16. _____

His birthday is March 4.

17. _____

I invite you. (plural, informal)

18. _____

Best wishes on your birthday! (singular, informal)

19. _____

Happy Easter!

20. _____

SCORE ☐

TOTAL SCORE ☐

KAPITEL 11 — Der Geburtstag

Name _____ Klasse _____ Datum _____

Dritte Stufe

Alternative Quiz 11-3A
Maximum Score: 30

Grammar and Vocabulary

A. Give the German equivalents for the following words. Be sure to include the articles with the nouns. (6 points)

1. _____ calendar
2. _____ to give (a gift)
3. _____ perfume
4. _____ gift idea
5. _____ different
6. _____ bouquet of flowers

SCORE _____

B. What are you and your friend giving to whom for different occasions? Write the correct grammar form in the blank in each sentence. (12 points)

Sie schenkt 7. _____ Mädchen eine CD zum Namenstag.
  a. das   b. der   c. die   d. dem

Schenkst du 8. _____ Oma Pralinen zum Geburtstag?
  a. deiner   b. deine   c. deinem   d. dein

Ich schenke 9. _____ Mutter einen Blumenstrauß zum Muttertag.
  a. meine   b. meiner   c. meinen   d. meinem

Ich schenke 10. _____ Onkel einen Kalender zu Weihnachten.
  a. mein   b. meiner   c. meinen   d. meinem

Schenkst du 11. _____ Tante Parfüm?
  a. deine   b. deinem   c. deinen   d. deiner

Was schenkst du 12. _____ zum Vatertag?
  a. ihm   b. es   c. ihr   d. ihn

SCORE _____

German 1 Komm mit!, Chapter 11   Student Make-Up Assignments

Name _____ Klasse _____ Datum _____

Alternative Quiz 11-3A

C. Give the German equivalents for the following sentences. (12 points)

Heike has a gift idea!

13. _____

Maybe I'll give my sister a CD for Christmas.

14. _____

I'll probably give my aunt jewelry for her birthday.

15. _____

Uwe, what kind of present are you buying for the German teacher?

16. _____

I'll give my grandmother perfume.

17. _____

I'll give my grandfather a watch.

18. _____

SCORE ☐

TOTAL SCORE ☐

Name _____ Klasse _____ Datum _____

KAPITEL 12 Die Fete

Alternative Quiz 12-1A

Erste Stufe

Maximum Score: 40

Grammar and Vocabulary

A. Using the **du**-command forms, tell the rest of your group what they can do for the end-of-school party. (6 points)

Martin und Erwin, 1. _____! (den Rasen mähen)

Maria, 2. _____! (die Fenster putzen)

Heidi, 3. _____! (ein Pfund Bratwurst holen)

Gisela, 4. _____! (einkaufen gehen)

Erna, 5. _____! (die Blumen gießen)

Fritz, 6. _____! (das Brot beim Bäcker kaufen)

SCORE _____

B. Complete the following conversations by filling in the blanks with the correct form of the verb **können**, and correct article and pronoun forms. (16 points)

A: Erika, ist der Blumenstrauß für 7. _____ (your) Mutter?

B: Ja, er ist für 8. _____ . Ich habe auch einen Blumenstrauß für

9. _____ (my) Tante gekauft. Ich muss fragen, was ich für

10. _____ tun kann.

A: Frau Meier, was 11. _____ ich für 12. _____ tun?

B: Alexandra, du 13. _____ bitte für 14. _____ Frau Huber den

Müll sortieren.

A: Für 15. _____ (whom) 16. _____ ich irgendetwas tun?

B: Für 17. _____ (me) 18. _____ du das Geschirr spülen.

A: Tante Helga und Onkel Max, was 19. _____ ich für

20. _____ tun?

B: Du 21. _____ für 22. _____ (us) die Fenster putzen.

SCORE _____

German 1 Komm mit!, Chapter 12   Student Make-Up Assignments   **143**

Name _____ Klasse _____ Datum _____

Alternative Quiz 12-1A

C. What do you and your friends know about getting around in your town? Complete the following conversations by filling in the blanks with the correct forms of the verb **wissen**. (8 points)

A: Thomas, 23. _____ du, wie ich zum Supermarkt kommt?

B: Nein, Frau Utz, ich 24. _____ es leider nicht.

A: Antje und Sabine, 25. _____ ihr wie ich zum Bahnhof komme?

B: Ja, wir 26. _____ es. Du gehst am besten die Straße entlang bis zur Scholzgasse, dann links, und da ist er.

A: Frau Rauch, 27. _____ Sie vielleicht, wie der Herr Steininger zur Post kommt?

B: Ja, das 28. _____ ich.

A: Ulli, 29. _____ die Claudia, wie sie zu dir nach Hause kommt?

B: Ja, sie 30. _____ es schon.

SCORE ☐

D. What's cooking? Find out by filling in the blanks with the correct vocabulary word. (10 points)

Zuerst, erhitzt man ein bisschen 31. _____ (oil) in einer Pfanne [du kannst auch 32. _____ (shortening) verwenden]. Dazu zwei fein gehackte 33. _____ (onions) geben, und bei mittlerer Hitze goldbraun braten. Den Saft einer 34. _____ (lemon) darüber spritzen, mit 35. _____ (salt) abschmecken und über die Käsespätzle streuen.

SCORE ☐

TOTAL SCORE ☐

Kapitel 12 — Die Fete

Zweite Stufe

Alternative Quiz 12-2A
Maximum Score: 30

Grammar and Vocabulary

A. You are asking a friend about his family and about what he is giving various family members as gifts. Complete the following sentences by filling in the blanks with the correct form of the appropriate possessive adjective, or the correct pronoun. (12 points)

A: Wie heißt 1. _____ Mutter?

B: 2. _____ heißt Klara.

A: Was schenkst du 3. _____ zum Muttertag?

B: Ich schenke 4. _____ Mutter Schmuck. Ich werde auch für

5. _____ die Fenster putzen.

A: Wie heißt 6. _____ Opa?

B: 7. _____ heißt Herr Fieser.

A: Was schenkst du 8. _____ zum Geburtstag?

B: Ich habe 9. _____ eine Armbanduhr gekauft. Ich werde auch für

10. _____ den Rasen mähen.

A: Was schenkst du 11. _____ Kusine zu Weihnachten?

B: Ich schenke 12. _____ eine CD.

SCORE _____

Name _____ Klasse _____ Datum _____

Alternative Quiz 12-2A

B. You and your friends are making plans to go places during spring break. Complete the sentences by filling in the blanks with the correct form of the verb **wollen** or the verb **müssen,** and the correct word (and its article when necessary). Each word has its own blank. (18 points)

CLAUDIA Ahmet, die Barbara und ich 13. _____ in

14. _____ 15. _____ gehen. (to the zoo)

16. _____ du mitkommen?

AHMET Nein, leider 17. _____ ich meinen Eltern helfen.

UDO Was soll ich nur in Berlin machen? Vielleicht werde ich

18. _____ 19. _____

20. _____ . (visit the city) Nein, ich möchte lieber

21. _____ 22. _____ . (ice skate) Paul und

Herbert, 23. _____ ihr mitkommen?

PAUL Ja, gerne! Aber zuerst 24. _____ wir das Zimmer aufräumen.

ELKE Unsere Lehrerin, Frau Krämer 25. _____ jeden Tag

26. _____ ! (jog) Sie hat viel Energie.

TOMAS Hallo, Frau Krämer! 27. _____ Sie mit uns in

28. _____ 29. _____ (to the park) gehen,

oder 30. _____ Sie lieber woanders joggen?

SCORE ☐

TOTAL SCORE ☐

146 Student Make-Up Assignments German 1 Komm mit!, Chapter 12

Name _____ Klasse _____ Datum _____

KAPITEL 12 Die Fete

Dritte Stufe

Alternative Quiz 12-3A

Maximum Score: 30

Grammar and Vocabulary

A. What furniture is in your house? Complete the following sentences by filling in the blanks with the correct vocabulary words and the correct pronouns. (18 points)

Letzte Woche habe ich ein **1.** _____ (sofa) für mein Zimmer gekauft;

2. _____ ist aus Leder. Ein **3.** _____ (table)

4. _____ (made of wood) steht davor. **5.** _____ ist

schön. (refers to the table) **6.** _____ ist auch **7.** _____

(modern) und **8.** _____ (with corners).

In **9.** _____ **10.** _____ (our living room) haben wir

einen **11.** _____ . (armchair) **12.** _____ ist aus

13. _____ (plastic). Wir haben **14.** _____ in die Ecke

gestellt. Weil wir gern lesen, steht **15.** _____ (a lamp) daneben.

16. _____ ist klein, aber schön.

In der Küche ist **17.** _____ (a sink). **18.** _____ ist nicht

groß. (refers to the sink)

SCORE ____

B. Complete the following sentences by filling in the blanks with the correct past tense form of the verb given in parentheses. (6 points)

Max **19.** _____ am Wochenende in München. (to be)

Dort hat er viel **20.** _____ . (to see)

Er hat einen Ausflug zum Chiemsee **21.** _____ . (to make)

Er hat seiner Kusine ein Buch über München **22.** _____ . (to buy)

Das Buch hat er im Zug **23.** _____ . (to read)

Danach hat er mit mir lang darüber **24.** _____ . (to speak)

SCORE ____

German 1 Komm mit!, Chapter 12   Student Make-Up Assignments **147**

Name _____ Klasse _____ Datum _____

Alternative Quiz 12-3A

C. Your mother has invited several of your friends to dinner. She is asking whether they would like more of what she is serving. They respond that they don't want any more. Complete the questions by filling in the blanks with a **möchte**-form. Complete the answers by filling in the correct form of **kein**. (6 points)

MUTTER Heiner, 25. _____ du noch Salat?

HEINER Nein, danke, 26. _____ Salat mehr.

MUTTER Maria, 27. _____ du noch Milch?

MARIA Nein, danke, 28. _____ Milch mehr.

MUTTER Frau Imke, 29. _____ Sie noch Torte?

FRAU IMKE Nein, danke, 30. _____ Torte mehr.

SCORE [ ]

TOTAL SCORE [ ]

Answer Key

Answers to Alternative Quizzes 1-1A, 1-2A, 1-3A

ANSWERS Alternative Quiz 1-1A

A. (5 points; 1 point per item)
Answers will vary. Possible answers:
1. Auf Wiedersehen!
2. Tag!; Hallo!
3. Tschüs!; Tschau!; Bis dann!
4. Guten Tag!; Guten Morgen!
5. Tag!; Hallo! Grüß dich!

B. (6 points; one point per item)
6. Grüß
7. Hallo
8. heißt
9. Sie
10. Wer
11. Ja

C. (14 points; 2 points per item)
12. heiße
13. heißt
14. heißt
15. Heißt
16. heißt
17. Heißt
18. heiße

D. (10 points; 2 points per item)
19. Wer ist das?
20. Sie heißt Sabine.
21. Wie heißt er?
22. Heißt er Ludwig?
23. Nein, der Junge heißt Paul.

ANSWERS Alternative Quiz 1-2A

A. (11 points; 1 point per item)
1. dreizehn
2. neun
3. null
4. vier
5. siebzehn
6. fünf
7. fünfzehn
8. elf
9. acht
10. Hauptstadt
11. Bundesland

B. (12 points; 2 points per item)
12. bist
13. ist
14. ist
15. bist
16. bin
17. sind

C. (4 points; 1 point per item)
18. ich
19. Wie
20. Das
21. Jahre

D. (8 points; 2 points per item)
22. Ist Manuela schon sechzehn Jahre alt?
23. Sind Vivian und Angelika neunzehn Jahre alt?
24. Wie alt bin ich? Ich bin siebzehn.
25. Bist du auch schon zwölf Jahre alt?

ANSWERS Alternative Quiz 1-3A

A. (10 points; 1 point per item)
1. kommst
2. neu
3. Wie
4. heißt
5. fünfzehn
6. heiße
7. komme
8. ist
9. alt
10. kommt

B. (12 points; 3 points per item)
11. Friedrich und Ulrike kommen mit dem Rad zur Schule.
12. Wie kommt sie zur Schule? Mit dem Auto?
13. Kommst du zu Fuß zur Schule?
14. Ich komme mit dem Moped zur Schule, und Ingrid kommt mit der U-Bahn zur Schule.

C. (8 points; 2 points per item)
Answers will vary. Possible answers:
Sie heißt Sara. Sie ist achtzehn Jahre alt. Sie kommt aus München. Sie kommt mit dem Auto zur Schule.

Answers to Alternative Quizzes 2-1A, 2-2A, 2-3A

ANSWERS Alternative Quiz 2-1A

A. (12 points; 2 points per item)
1. Klavier
2. Gitarre
3. Volleyball
4. Fußball
5. Karten
6. Schach

B. (8 points; 1 point per item)
7. Spielt
8. machst
9. spielt
10. mache
11. spiele
12. macht
13. spielt
14. Machst

C. (10 points; 2 points per item)
15. Was macht Manuela?
16. Sie spielt Schach.
17. Sie spielt nicht Karten.
18. Macht Udo Sport?
19. Ja, er spielt Tennis und Fußball.

ANSWERS Alternative Quiz 2-2A

A. (20 points; 2 points per item)
1. Ich wandere gern.
2. Heike und Gisela basteln nicht gern.
3. Schwimmt ihr oft?
4. Ihr sammelt gern Briefmarken.
5. Er zeichnet nicht gern.
6. Besucht sie gern Freunde?
7. Du hörst sehr gern Musik.
8. Ich tanze nicht gern.
9. Schauen sie nicht gern Fernsehen?
10. Wir wandern gern.

B. (10 points; 2 points per item)
11. Sammelst du
12. Wandert ihr
13. Schreiben Sie
14. Schwimmst du
15. Basteln Sie

C. (5 points; 2.5 points per item)
Answers will vary. Possible answers:
16. Ich spiele gern Schach und ich schaue gern Fernsehen.
17. Ich spiele nicht gern Karten und ich spiele nicht so gern Fußball.

ANSWERS Alternative Quiz 2-3A

A. (12 points; 1 point per item)
1. h
2. i
3. g
4. j
5. l
6. a
7. d
8. e
9. c
10. k
11. b
12. f

B. (8 points; 1 point per item)
13. segelt
14. tanzt
15. findet
16. bastle
17. Sammelst
18. Wandert
19. schwimme
20. findest

C. (15 points; 3 points per item)
Answers will vary. Possible answers:
21. Findest du Briefmarken sammeln interessant, Sara?
22. Was macht ihr nach der Schule, Barbara und Inge?
23. Im Sommer wandere ich.
24. Sie findet Schach prima. Das finde ich auch.
25. Inge und Peter wandern am Wochenende.

Answers to Alternative Quizzes 3-1A, 3-2A, 3-3A

ANSWERS Alternative Quiz 3-1A

A. (8 points; 1 point per item)
1. mit dem Auto
2. wohnt
3. ein Vorort von
4. wohnst
5. in der Nähe
6. zu Fuß
7. Wohnen
8. in der Stadt

B. (12 points; 1 point per item)
9. möchte
10. ein Glas Orangensaft
11. möchten
12. ein Stück Kuchen
13. möchten
14. ein paar Kekse
15. möchte
16. eine Limo
17. Möchtest
18. eine Cola
19. möchten
20. Obst

C. (15 points; 3 points per item)
Answers will vary. Possible answers:
21. Manfred und Holger, wohnt ihr weit von hier?
22. Ja, wir wohnen in der Brunnen Straße.
23. Sie möchte ein paar Kekse.
24. Ich möchte ein Glas Apfelsaft, und er möchte eine Cola.
25. A: Danke (sehr)! B: Bitte (sehr)!

ANSWERS Alternative Quiz 3-2A

A. (4 points; 1 point per item)
1. alt
2. schön
3. bequem
4. groß

B. (16 points; 2 points per item)
5. der Stuhl
6. das Regal
7. das Bett
8. der Schreibtisch
9. der Schrank
10. das Zimmer
11. die Stereoanlage
12. die Möbel; X

C. (10 points; 2 points per item)
13. Es ist unbequem.
14. Sie ist kaputt.
15. Sie sind neu.
16. Er ist klein.
17. Er ist hässlich.

ANSWERS Alternative Quiz 3-3A

A. (10 points; 1 point per item)
1. vierundsechzig
2. zweiundfünfzig
3. siebenundzwanzig
4. neunundneunzig
5. sechsundachtzig
6. vierundvierzig
7. einunddreißig
8. hundert
9. fünfundzwanzig
10. dreiundsiebzig

B. (15 points; 1 point per item)
11. sein
12. seine
13. seine
14. seine
15. sein
16. sein
17. seine
18. deine
19. meine
20. meine
21. mein
22. ihr
23. ihr
24. sein
25. seine

C. (10 points; 2 points per item)
26. Meine Tante hat lange rote Haare und braune Augen.
27. Seine Mutter hat kurze schwarze Haare.
28. Dein Onkel Otto hat eine Glatze und eine Brille, und er ist 46 Jahre alt.
29. Wie sieht ihr Cousin aus?
30. Wie heißen Ilse's Großeltern?

Answers to Alternative Quizzes 4-1A, 4-2A, 4-3A

ANSWERS Alternative Quiz 4-1A

A. (9 points; 1 point per item)
1. Erdkunde
2. Kunst
3. Dienstag
4. Geschichte
5. Freitag
6. Samstag
7. Bio (Biologie)
8. Chemie
9. Sonntag

B. (10 points; 1 point per item)
10. habt
11. haben
12. hat
13. hat
14. hast
15. habe
16. hat
17. hat
18. habe
19. Hast

C. (8 points; 2 points per item)
Answers will vary. Possible answers:
20. Zuerst habe ich Mathe.
21. Dann habe ich Chemie.
22. Danach habe ich Erdkunde.
23. Zuletzt habe ich Physik.

D. (8 points; 2 points per item)
Answers will vary. Possible answers:
24. Ich habe Englisch um elf Uhr.
25. Um acht Uhr habe ich Bio.
26. Am Freitag habe ich Deutsch, Mathe, Religion und Englisch.
27. Am Dienstag habe ich Biologie, Deutsch, Mathe und Erdkunde.

ANSWERS Alternative Quiz 4-2A

A. (16 points; 2 points per item)
Answers will vary. Possible answers:
1. Herr Setzer, haben Sie Fußball gern?
2. Erdkunde ist mein Lieblingsfach.
3. Udo und Jens haben Physik nicht gern.
4. Wir haben Kunst gern.
5. Manuela und Erika, habt ihr Englisch gern?
6. Sie hat Sport gern.
7. Peter, ist Claudia deine Lieblingskusine?
8. Sie hat Deutsch nicht gern.

B. (8 points; 2 points per item)
Answers will vary. Possible answers:
9. Spitze!
10. Prima!
11. Schade!
12. So ein Pech!

C. (6 points; 1.5 points per item)
Answers will vary. Possible answers:
13. Ich habe eine Eins in Erdkunde.
14. Toll!
15. Ich habe eine Fünf in Physik.
16. Schlecht!

ANSWERS Alternative Quiz 4-3A

A. (12 points; 2 points per item)
1. der Radiergummi, die Radiergummis
2. das Buch, die Bücher
3. der Taschenrechner, die Taschenrechner
4. das Wörterbuch, die Wörterbücher
5. der Bleistift, die Bleistifte
6. die Schultasche, die Schultaschen

B. (5 points; 1 point per item)
7. billig
8. EUR 50 / 50 Euro
9. Das ist preiswert.
10. teuer
11. nur 3 Euro / nur EUR 3

C. (10 points; 1 point per item)
12. kostet
13. es
14. Es
15. kostet
16. kostet
17. Sie
18. kostet
19. kosten
20. Sie
21. kosten

D. (8 points; 2 points per item)
Answers will vary. Possible answers:
22. Schau mal! Die Hefte sind dort.
23. Die Wörterbücher sind da hinten.
24. Die Kulis sind hier vorn.
25. Sind die Schulsachen dort drüben?

Answers to Alternative Quizzes 5-1A, 5-2A, 5-3A

ANSWERS Alternative Quiz 5-1A

A. (7 points; 1 point per item)
1. dunkelblau
2. gelb
3. schwarz
4. braun
5. rot
6. grün
7. weiß

B. (7 points; 1 point per item)
8. Hose
9. Hemd
10. Pulli
11. Pulli
12. Hemd
13. Hemd
14. Hose

C. (10 points; 1 point per item)
15. Der
16. der
17. Das
18. die
19. einen
20. Die
21. die
22. die
23. die
24. den

D. (11 points; 1 point per item)
25. einen
26. eine
27. -
28. einen
29. Ein
30. ein
31. -
32. eine
33. Ein
34. Ein
35. -

ANSWERS Alternative Quiz 5-2A

A. (15 points; 3 points per item)
1. Es passt nicht.
2. Ich bin nicht sicher.
3. Es ist ein bisschen eng.
4. Nein, es ist teuer.
5. Ich finde es echt stark.

B. (5 points; 1 point per item)
6. zu klein
7. zu eng
8. zu groß
9. zu kurz
10. zu lang

C. (10 points; 1 point per item)
11. deine
12. passen
13. Blau
14. fesch
15. gefällt
16. weiß
17. du
18. zu eng
19. überhaupt
20. prima

D. (5 points; 1 point per item)
21. er
22. ihn
23. sie
24. ihn
25. er

ANSWERS Alternative Quiz 5-3A

A. (6 points; 2 points per item)
1. Seine Turnschuhe sehen lässig aus.
2. Ute zieht ihren Jogging-Anzug an.
3. Du probierst die blaue Jacke an.

B. (12 points; 2 points per item)
4. sieht...aus
5. nimmst
6. nehme
7. nimmt
8. nimmt
9. sieht...aus

C. (6 points; 1 point per item)
10. du
11. weiß
12. Klamotten
13. brauche
14. Bluse
15. *Modehaus Bügelfrei*

D. (6 points; 1 point per item)
16. Antje
17. Ulrike
18. Ulrike
19. Antje
20. Monika
21. Monika

Answers to Alternative Quizzes 6-1A, 6-2A, 6-3A

ANSWERS Alternative Quiz 6-1A

A. (5 points; 1 point per item)
1. Wie geht's?
2. Miserabel!
3. Es geht.
4. Schlecht.
5. Sehr gut!

B. (10 points; 1 point per item)
6. g
7. a
8. b
9. j
10. h
11. f
12. c
13. e
14. i
15. d

C. (10 points; 2 points per item)
Answers will vary. Possible answers:
16. Viertel nach zehn
17. halb zehn
18. Viertel vor zwölf
19. halb drei
20. Viertel vor zwei

D. (5 points; 1 point per item)
21. um Viertel vor zehn
22. um halb elf
23. um halb zwei
24. um Viertel nach elf
25. um acht

ANSWERS Alternative Quiz 6-2A

A. (5 points; 1 point per item)
1. in die Stadt
2. in ein Café/ins Café
3. ins Kino
4. ins Schwimmbad
5. in ein Konzert

B. (12 points; 2 points per item)
6. willst
7. will
8. Willst
9. will
10. wollen
11. willst

C. (10 points; 1 point per item)
12. zuerst
13. Donnerstag
14. Dann
15. gehe
16. nach Hause
17. Hausaufgaben
18. besuche
19. meine
20. hören
21. Karten

D. (8 points; 2 points per item)
Answers will vary. Possible answers:
22. Wir wollen Fußball spielen.
23. Markus und Udo wollen Eis essen.
24. Willst du in die Stadt gehen?
25. Wann will Heike die Hausaufgaben machen?

ANSWERS Alternative Quiz 6-3A

A. (10 points; 2 points per item)
Answers will vary. Possible answers:
1. Wie schmeckt's?
2. Ich will möchte/will zahlen!
3. Das macht (zusammen) EUR 13,50.
4. Pass auf!
5. Sagenhaft!

B. (10 points; 1 point per item)
6. ein
7. ein
8. ein
9. eine
10. eine
11. ein
12. eine
13. eine
14. einen
15. ein

C. (5 points; 1 point per item)
16. d
17. c
18. e
19. a
20. b

D. (10 points; 1 point per item)
21. machst
22. gehe
23. Willst
24. esse
25. bekomme
26. schmeckt
27. zahlen
28. Stimmt
29. kaufen
30. brauche

Answers to Alternative Quizzes 7-1A, 7-2A, 7-3A

ANSWERS Alternative Quiz 7-1A

A. (15 points; 1 point per item)
1. Klamotten
2. sauge
3. gieße
4. spüle
5. Staub
6. decke
7. helfe
8. mein Zimmer
9. putze
10. mache
11. die Katze
12. die Blumen
13. füttere
14. sortiere
15. mähe

B. (6 points; 1 point per item)
16. musst
17. muss.....sortieren
18. müssen
19. müssen.....mähen
20. muss
21. musst.....aufräumen

C. (3 points; 1 point per item)
Answers will vary. Possible answers:
22. Bruno räumt den Tisch ab.
23. Marolda räumt das Zimmer auf.
24. Peter probiert das Hemd an.

D. (6 points; 2 points per item)
25. Das geht nicht.
26. Ich kann leider nicht.
25. Komm doch mit!

Answers Alternative Quiz 7-2A

A. (10 points; 2 points per item)
1. ungefähr dreimal im Monat
2. jeden Tag
3. fünfmal in der Woche
4. zweimal im Monat
5. Wie oft?

B. (10 points; 2 points per item)
6. kann.....aufräumen
7. könnt.....putzen
8. kann.....mähen
9. könnt.....gießen
10. kannst.....füttern

C. (10 points; 2 points per item)
11. Die Blumen sind für sie.
12. Der Apfelkuchen ist für uns.
13. Die neue Hose ist für dich.
14. Die Pizza ist für mich.
15. Der Tisch ist für euch.

D. (10 points; 1 point per item)
16. können
17. dich
18. könnt
19. mich
20. mähen
21. kannst
22. füttern
23. kann
24. sortieren
25. putzen

ANSWERS Alternative Quiz 7-3A

A. (10 points; 2 points per item)
Answers will vary. Possible answers.
1. Im August ist es heiß und trocken.
2. Wie ist das Wetter im März?
3. Im Januar ist es kalt und nass.
4. Wie viel Grad haben wir?
5. Heute regnet es.

B. (5 points; 1 point per item)
6. c
7. d
8. e
9. b
10. a

C. (5 points; 1 point per item)
11. b
12. e
13. a
14. c
15. d

D. (10 points; 1 point per item)
16. das Wetter
17. der Wetterbericht
18. sehr heiß
19. regnet
20. heute
21. kühl
22. 20 Grad
23. trocken
24. baden
25. Schwimmbad

German 1 Komm mit!, Chapter 7   Student Make-Up Assignments

Answers to Alternative Quizzes 8-1A, 8-2A, 8-3A

ANSWERS Alternative Quiz 8-1A

A. (10 points; 1 point per item)
1. soll
2. dich
3. Brot
4. Bäcker
5. Torte
6. geh
7. ein Hähnchen
8. Gemüseladen
9. kauf
10. EUR 20

B. (10 points; 1 point per item)
11. den
12. den
13. die
14. die
15. das
16. die
17. die
18. die
19. die
20. das

C. (5 points; 1 point per item)
21. c
22. a
23. b
24. d
25. e

D. (5 points; 1 point per item)
26. im Café
27. im Obst- und Gemüseladen
28. beim Bäcker
29. beim Metzger
30. im Supermarkt

ANSWERS Alternative Quiz 8-2A

A. (5 points; 1 point per item)
1. helfen
2. Haben
3. noch
4. etwas
5. alles

B. (5 points; 1 point per item)
6. Käse und Butter
7. ein Kilo Kartoffeln
8. 250 Gramm Aufschnitt
9. einen Liter Milch
10. zwei Pfund Trauben

C. (15 points; 3 points per item)
Answers will vary. Possible answers:
11. Haben Sie noch einen Wunsch?
12. Ich brauche noch ein Pfund Hackfleisch.
13. Wie viele Semmeln kaufst du beim Bäcker?
14. Ich brauche ein bisschen mehr Mehl.
15. Das ist alles. Danke!

D. (10 points; 1 point per item)
16. die
17. Sie
18. der
19. Er
20. die
21. Sie
22. der
23. Er
24. die
25. Sie

ANSWERS Alternative Quiz 8-3A

A. (5 points; 1 point per item)
1. c
2. d
3. e
4. b
5. a

B. (15 points; 3 points per item)
Answers will vary. Possible answers:
6. Gestern Abend waren wir im Kino.
7. Heute Nachmittag war er beim Metzger.
8. Vorgestern war ich zu Hause.
9. Heike muss morgen einkaufen gehen, weil sie Milch braucht.
10. Letztes Wochenende waren sie in Berlin.

C. (10 points; 1 point per item)
11. waren
12. gestern Abend
13. war
14. im Kino
15. Film
16. *Gladiator*
17. wie viel
18. halb
19. waren
20. waren

D. (5 points; 1 point per item)
21. Heidi war in der *Boutique Schick,* weil dort die Blusen preiswert sind.
22. Peter geht heute ins Schwimmbad, weil es sehr heiß ist.
23. Ich war gestern nicht in der Schule, weil ich krank war.
24. Sie geht nicht ins Kino, weil sie kein Geld hat.
25. Antje hat die Semmeln beim Bäcker gekauft, weil sie dort frisch sind.

Answers to Alternative Quizzes 9-1A, 9-2A, 9-3A

ANSWERS Alternative Quiz 9-1A

A. (5 points; 1 point per item)
1. the garden
2. the city hall
3. the market square
4. the church
5. the museum

B. (10 points; 1 point per item)
6. wisst
7. wissen
8. weißt
9. weiß
10. Wissen
11. wissen
12. Weiß
13. weiß
14. wissen
15. weiß

C. (15 points; 3 points per item)
Answers will vary. Possible answers:
16. Anneliese, weißt du, wo die Kirche ist?
17. Markus und Erika, wisst ihr, wo die Post ist?
18. Frau Hinterhofer, wissen Sie, wo das Hotel ist?
19. Max, weißt du, wo das Theater ist?
20. Herr Hinterhuber, wissen Sie, wo die Bank ist?

ANSWERS Alternative Quiz 9-2A

A. (16 points; 2 points per item)
1. Gehen
2. Fahr
3. Fahr
4. Fahren
5. Fahren
6. fahren
7. Geht
8. geht

B. (6 points; 1 point per item)
9. Gehen Sie
10. zur
11. Fahr
12. zur
13. Fahrt
14. zum

C. (13 points; 1 point per item)
15. zum
16. Geht
17. zum
18. geht
19. geht
20. zur
21. geht
22. Gehen
23. zum
24. gehen
25. Geh
26. zur
27. zur

ANSWERS Alternative Quiz 9-3A

A. (12 points; 1 point per item)
1. noch eine
2. Wurst
3. noch einen
4. Apfelsaft
5. noch ein
6. Mineralwasser
7. noch ein
8. Eis
9. noch eine
10. Semmel
11. noch ein
12. Gyros

B. (7 points; 1 point per item)
13. Gibt es
14. es gibt
15. gibt es
16. gibt es
17. Gibt es
18. Es gibt
19. Es gibt

C. (8 points; 2 points per item)
20. keinen
21. keine
22. keine
23. keine

D. (8 points; 2 points per item)
24. es noch Kartoffeln gibt.
25. der Holger im Supermarkt war.
26. es heute Eis gibt.
27. die Elfriede zum Gemüseladen geht.

Answers to Alternative Quizzes 10-1A, 10-2A, 10-3A

ANSWERS Alternative Quiz 10-1A

A. (10 points; 1 point per item)
1. Kennt
2. Weißt
3. Wissen
4. Weiß
5. Kennen
6. Kennst
7. kenne
8. kennst
9. weißt
10. Wisst

B. (9 points; 3 points per item)
Answers will vary. Possible answers:
11. Marolda, magst du klassische Musik?
12. Albert, was für Filme magst du?
13. Heino, magst du Kriegsfilme?

C. (15 points; 1 point per item)
14. mögen
15. Komödien
16. Liebesfilme
17. magst
18. mag
19. Horrorfilme
20. Krimis
21. mögt
22. mögen
23. Abenteuerfilme
24. mögen
25. Sciencefictionfilme
26. Mögen
27. Western
28. Horrorfilme

D. (6 points; 1 point per item)
29. den Film
30. den Schauspieler
31. die Schauspielerin
32. die Sängerin
33. die Gruppe
34. das Lied

ANSWERS Alternative Quiz 10-2A

A. (14 points; 2 points per item)
1. sieht
2. sieht
3. seht
4. sehe
5. sehen
6. sehen
7. siehst

B. (6 points; 2 points per item)
8. gern
9. lieber
10. am liebsten

C. (10 points; 1 point per item)
11. schlecht
12. phantasievoll
13. spannend
14. sensationell
15. dumm
16. schmalzig
17. traurig
18. grausam
19. brutal
20. lustig

ANSWERS Alternative Quiz 10-3A

A. (7 points; 1 point per item)
1. liest
2. liest
3. lest
4. liest
5. lesen
6. liest
7. lesen

B. (5 points; 1 point per item)
8. waren
9. gemacht
10. gesehen
11. gesprochen
12. gelesen

C. (18 points; 2 points per item)
13. Worüber sprichst du?
14. Worüber sprecht ihr?
15. Ich spreche über Politik.
16. Uwe spricht über den Abenteuerfilm.
17. Meine Eltern sprechen über das Wetter.
18. Wir sprechen über Mode.
19. Sie sprechen über die Umwelt.
20. Über wen sprecht ihr?
21. Elke spricht über den Gruselroman.

Answers to Alternative Quizzes 11-1A, 11-2A, 11-3A

ANSWERS Alternative Quiz 11-1A

A. (8 points; 1 point per item)
1. anrufe
2. Rufst
3. an
4. rufe
5. an
6. rufen
7. an
8. anrufen

B. (10 points; 1 point per item)
9. Telefonieren
10. in die Telefonzelle gehen
11. den Hörer abheben
12. die Münzen einstecken
13. die Telefonnummer wählen
14. den Apparat
15. Kann
16. sprechen
17. besetzt
18. den Hörer auflegen

C. (12 points; 3 points per item)
19. Auf Wiederhören!
20. Einen Moment, bitte!
21. Hier bei Blum.
22. Hier ist Frau Hinterhuber.

ANSWERS Alternative Quiz 11-2A

A. (20 points; 2 points per item)
1. zwölften Oktober
2. siebten März
3. achten Mai
4. fünfundzwanzigsten Februar
5. siebzehnten Juli
6. achten August
7. achtundzwanzigsten Juni
8. elften April
9. siebten Dezember
10. fünfzehnten März

B. (20 points; 2 points per item)
11. Alles Gute zum Geburtstag!
12. Alles Gute zum Muttertag!
13. Alles Gute zum Vatertag!
14. Frohes Chanukka-Fest!
15. Wann hat sie Geburtstag?
16. Fröhliche Weihnachten!
17. Er hat am vierten März Geburtstag.
18. Ich lade euch ein.
19. Herzlichen Glückwunsch zum Geburtstag!
20. Frohe Ostern!

ANSWERS Alternative Quiz 11-3A

A. (6 points; 1 point per item)
1. der Kalender
2. schenken
3. das Parfüm
4. die Geschenkidee
5. verschieden
6. der Blumenstrauß

B. (12 points; 2 points per item)
7. d
8. a
9. b
10. d
11. d
12. a

C. (12 points; 2 points per item)
Answers will vary. Possible answers:
13. Heike hat eine Geschenkidee!
14. Vielleicht schenke ich meiner Schwester eine CD zu Weihnachten.
15. Wahrscheinlich schenke ich meiner Tante Schmuck zum Geburtstag.
16. Uwe, was für ein Geschenk kaufst du dem Deutschlehrer?
17. Ich schenke meiner Oma Parfüm.
18. Ich schenke meinem Opa eine Armbanduhr.

Answers to Alternative Quizzes 12-1A, 12-2A, 12-3A

ANSWERS Alternative Quiz 12-1A

A. (6 points; 1 point per item)
1. mäht den Rasen
2. putz die Fenster
3. hol ein Pfund Bratwurst
4. geh einkaufen
5. gieß die Blumen
6. kauf das Brot beim Bäcker

B. (16 points; 1 point per item)
7. deine
8. sie
9. meine
10. sie
11. kann
12. Sie
13. kannst
14. die
15. wen
16. kann
17. mich
18. kannst
19. kann
20. euch
21. kannst
22. uns

C. (8 points; 1 point per item)
23. weißt
24. weiß
25. wisst
26. wissen
27. wissen
28. weiß
29. weiß
30. weiß

D. (10 points; 2 points per item)
31. Öl
32. Butterschmalz
33. Zwiebeln
34. Zitrone
35. Salz

ANSWERS Alternative Quiz 12-2A

A. (12 points; 1 point per item)
1. deine
2. Sie
3. ihr
4. meiner
5. sie
6. dein
7. Er
8. ihm
9. ihm
10. ihn
11. deiner
12. ihr

B. (18 points; 1 point per item)
13. wollen
14. den
15. Zoo
16. Willst
17. muss
18. die
19. Stadt
20. besichtigen
21. Schlittschuh
22. laufen
23. wollt
24. müssen
25. will
26. joggen
27. Wollen
28. den
29. Park
30. wollen

ANSWERS Alternative Quiz 12-3A

A. (18 points; 1 point per item)
1. Sofa
2. Es
3. Tisch
4. aus Holz
5. Er
6. Er
7. modern
8. eckig
9. unserem
10. Wohnzimmer
11. Sessel
12. Er
13. Kunststoff
14. ihn
15. eine Lampe
16. Sie
17. ein Spülbecken
18. Es

B. (6 points; 1 point per item)
19. war
20. gesehen
21. gemacht
22. gekauft
23. gelesen
24. gesprochen

C. (6 points; 1 point per item)
25. möchtest
26. keinen
27. möchtest
28. keine
29. möchten
30. keine